ASTROLOGY and YOU

JULIA *and* DEREK PARKER

DORLING KINDERSLEY
London • New York • Stuttgart • Moscow

To you, the reader, who we hope will look further

A DORLING KINDERSLEY BOOK

Project Editor • Tracie Lee Davis
Art Editor • Anna Benjamin
Editors • Annabel Morgan, Sarah Wilde
Designer • Wendy Bartlet
Senior Editor • Sharon Lucas
Senior Art Editor • Tim Scott
Managing Editor • Francis Ritter
Managing Art Editor • Derek Coombes
DTP Designers • Cressida Joyce, Sonia Charbonnier
Production Controller • Ruth Charlton
Picture Researcher • Louise Thomas

First published in Great Britain in 1997 by
Dorling Kindersley Limited, 9 Henrietta Street, London WC2E 8PS

Visit us on the World Wide Web at http://www.dk.com

Copyright © 1997 Dorling Kindersley Limited, London
Text copyright © 1997 Julia and Derek Parker
The right of Julia and Derek Parker to be identified as Writers of this Work has been
asserted by them in accordance with the Copyright, Designs, and Patents Act 1988.

A CIP catalogue record for this pack is available from the British Library.

Reproduced by Bright Arts, Hong Kong

*Astrology and You, Planetary Tables, Instructions, Ascendant Chart, Midheaven Chart, Traditional Factors/
Moon Charts,* and *Sticker Sheets* printed in Hong Kong by Wing King Tong Co., Ltd.

Air/Fire Wheel, Earth/Water Wheel, Birth Chart, Acetate Sheet, and *Box*
printed and assembled in China by New Island Printing Co., Ltd.

CONTENTS

Introduction 4

The Planets through the Signs 7
The Sun through the Signs 8
The Moon through the Signs 20
Mercury through the Signs 24
Venus through the Signs 28
Mars through the Signs 32
Jupiter through the Signs 36
Saturn through the Signs 40
Uranus through the Signs 44
Neptune through the Signs 48
Pluto through the Signs 50

The Planets through the Houses 53
The Sun through the Houses 54
The Moon through the Houses 56
Mercury through the Houses 58
Venus through the Houses 60

Mars through the Houses 62
Jupiter through the Houses 64
Saturn through the Houses 66
Uranus through the Houses 68
Neptune through the Houses 70
Pluto through the Houses 72

The Aspects 75
The Aspects of the Sun 76
The Moon's Influence 80
The Aspects of Mercury 82
The Aspects of Venus 85
The Aspects of Mars 88
The Aspects of Jupiter 90
The Aspects of Saturn 92
The Aspects of Uranus,
Neptune, and Pluto 94

Acknowledgments 96

INTRODUCTION

THIS PACK PROVIDES a complete introduction to astrology. It takes you several steps further than simple Sun-sign astrology, and includes all the information you will need to construct and interpret your own birth chart, and the birth charts of your friends and family.

Most people realize that the twelve Sun signs, which mark the time during the year when you are born, play only a very small part in astrology. A professional astrologer will construct a birth chart, which is a map of the skies at the time and place of your birth. Not only the Sun, but the position of every planet is plotted precisely, so that each planet's influence on your life can be calculated.

Nevertheless, everyone starts with the Sun sign, and when you read the analysis of your Sun-sign personality at the beginning of this book, you will no doubt identify with several of the character traits that you are supposed to possess. It used to be thought that your Sun sign revealed your internal self, the "you" that only your closest friends and relatives might know, while your Ascendant sign, which is the one that was rising over the eastern horizon at the moment you were born, showed the external "you", the one you present to the world. However,

Astrology and the Body
Each astrological sign is associated with an area of the body. The sign you were born under indicates where your body may be vulnerable to illness.

we believe that during the present century this theory has been reversed, and that your Sun sign now reveals your external characteristics. This may have come about because there has been such a strong interest in Sun-sign astrology since it was popularized by "the stars" appearing in newspapers in the 1920s. Everyone now knows some of the traits of their Sun sign, and may feel that they "ought" to exhibit them. But in fact, however much you recognize yourself as "a Leo" or "a Scorpio", this is only a small part of what astrology can reveal to you about yourself and other people. The signs that appear on your Ascendant and Midheaven, the positions of the other planets, and the angles they make to each other, known as aspects, are all crucial elements of the birth chart that combine to give you a complete picture of your personality.

Drawing up and interpreting a birth chart can be rather difficult, but, by using the material we have provided in this pack, you are spared having to do the actual calculations that astrologers usually have to learn, and are provided with short-cuts to help you compile your chart. The instructions booklet is designed to answer general queries that will arise, and the special factors that follow should also be borne in mind.

Finding latitude and longitude   Do not worry if you were not born close to one of the cities listed in the concertina charts, *How to Find Your Ascendant* and *How to Find Your Midheaven*. There is the strongest possibility that the co-ordinates for the city nearest your birthplace will be accurate enough for your purpose.

Your time of birth   If you do not know your time of birth, make all the calculations as though you were born at midday on your birthday. This means that you will not be able to discover your true Ascendant or Midheaven, and will have to ignore them when drawing and interpreting your chart. This type of chart is called a solar chart. You will be able to plot the Sun and the planets accurately, but will be unsure which houses the planets occupy.

Time anomalies   Remember to check whether daylight savings time, summer time, or war time was in operation at the time of your birth. Your local library can tell you this.

Born on the cusp   Amateur astrologers talk about being "born on the cusp", that is, with the Sun apparently poised on the dividing line between one sign and another. They mistakenly believe that these individuals will share the characteristics of two signs. In fact, the Sun moves from one sign into another with the accuracy of a stopwatch, and you will be either Aries or Taurus (for example), not a mixture of both. However, some people are born on the day the Sun changes signs. Unless they know exactly what time they were born, they may never know accurately under which Sun sign they were born, although an astrologer should be able to form an opinion by studying the person's character. If you do know your birth time accurately, but are unable to see where any planet falls on our tables, the safest thing is to consult a full ephemeris.

Finally, we must in fairness mention that, as with all short-cuts, this pack is limited in what it can teach you. It bears much the same

The Sun God
This 15th-century Italian illustration of the Sun god features the Lion, the symbol of Leo, which is ruled by the Sun.

relationship to a full course in astrology as a ready reckoner does to the whole body of mathematical theory! Sometimes you may disagree with an interpretation, and find yourself saying, "But that's just not me!" This could be because our method of plotting the Ascendant, for instance, is not as accurate as if you were using a complete ephemeris. If you really do not recognize yourself in an interpretation, read the section before and after the one to which you have been directed. For instance, if the interpretation for a Gemini Ascendant seems inaccurate, read those for Taurus and Cancer; one of them will strike you as the right one. You may also need to follow this procedure when considering the position of the Moon. However, as you begin to interpret your completed birth chart, you will most likely be delighted by its accuracy and fascinated by the insights you will gain into both your own and other people's personalities.

THE
PLANETS
THROUGH
THE SIGNS

At the moment of your birth, the Sun could be seen, from Earth, in a certain part of the sky. Centuries ago, astrologers divided the sky into twelve sections and gave each one a name – the twelve signs of the zodiac. Your Sun sign relates to the sign of the zodiac that the Sun was in on the day of your birth. The Sun remains in each of the twelve signs for approximately four weeks. Astrologers believe that the other planets in the solar system also have a powerful effect on your personality, depending on which sign of the zodiac they were in at the moment of your birth.

An astrological map that appeared in Harmonia Macro Cosmica *in 1660.*

PLANETS

SUN

MOON

MERCURY

VENUS

MARS

JUPITER

SATURN

URANUS

NEPTUNE

PLUTO

SIGNS

ARIES

TAURUS

GEMINI

CANCER

LEO

VIRGO

LIBRA

SCORPIO

SAGITTARIUS

THE SUN IN ARIES

ARIENS ARE DYNAMIC AND DETERMINED, IF SOMETIMES OVER-SWIFT IN THEIR REACTIONS. THEY ARE ENTHUSIASTIC AND CONFIDENT PEOPLE, WHO DEAL WITH EVERYDAY LIFE IN A MATTER-OF-FACT WAY. THEY HAVE AN ENVIABLE ABILITY TO GO STRAIGHT TO THE HEART OF ANY PROBLEM AND QUICKLY RESOLVE IT.

BASIC PERSONALITY

Ariens are adventurous and enthusiastic. They need to be achievers, to succeed in all of their aims, whether at work or socially, and can sometimes be selfish in attaining them. Lack of success affects them more than most people, and they are likely to become irritable and self-obsessed as a result.

Relationships Ariens tend to fall in love at first sight and can win hearts easily. Their partners must be lively, and quick to react to them intellectually and sexually. Ariens like to encourage their children, though impatience can make them unsympathetic. Arien children are extremely competitive and thrive best in a flexible, stimulating environment.

Career Ariens have good business minds, and can make money by combining caution with their keen sense of enterprise. Their lively minds make them especially good psychiatrists. Dentistry is also favoured.

Leisure Ariens' hobbies should include energetic sport, because they need plenty of exercise to keep in shape. They should beware of injury through over-enthusiasm. A love of spicy food can prove trying to the sensitive Arien digestion.

Traditional Associations
Aries is a fire sign and its ruling planet is Mars. It is a masculine sign and its symbol is the Ram.

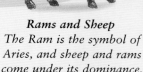

Rams and Sheep
The Ram is the symbol of Aries, and sheep and rams come under its dominance.

Thistle
Prickly shrubs such as the thistle are ruled by Aries.

Aries glyph

ARIES AS ASCENDANT

If Aries was rising at the time of birth, the urge to achieve will be a dominant force in the subject's life. During childhood this can lead to rivalry with siblings. Aries-Ascendant people find it particularly easy to adapt to circumstances, but may over-simplify the problems they face. It is advisable for them to cultivate the facility to look coolly and analytically at any difficulties they encounter, rather than make any rushed decisions. They thrive in a steady emotional relationship, and will strive to understand and support their partner.

ARIES AS MIDHEAVEN

When the Midheaven is Aries, Cancer or Leo will be in the Ascendant in northern latitudes. In southern latitudes, Gemini or Cancer will be the rising sign. Anyone with Aries as his or her Midheaven will aspire to be independent and assertive. When Gemini is rising, the individual is likely to express the Geminian ability for wheeling and dealing to achieve his or her own ends. If a subject has Cancer rising, the sensitivity of the rising sign means that his or her concern for other people will hinder success. Nevertheless, the attraction to Arien interests will be very powerful, and he or she will have the desire to be a big achiever. Assertiveness will be significantly enhanced if Leo is rising. These individuals tend to be very ambitious, and are likely to attain their goals.

Diamond
The diamond is an Arien gemstone.

PLANETS

SUN

MOON

MERCURY

VENUS

MARS

JUPITER

SATURN

URANUS

NEPTUNE

PLUTO

SIGNS

ARIES

TAURUS

GEMINI

CANCER

LEO

LIBRA

SCORPIO

SAGITTARIUS

CAPRICORN

AQUARIUS

PISCES

THE SUN IN TAURUS

TAUREANS ARE PATIENT AND RELIABLE. THEY NEED SECURITY IN EVERY AREA OF THEIR LIVES, WHICH CAN MAKE THEM POSSESSIVE IN PERSONAL RELATIONSHIPS. RELIABILITY IS PERHAPS THEIR MOST REMARKABLE QUALITY, AND THEIR COMMON SENSE CAN BE INVALUABLE. THEIR NATURAL CHARM MAKES THEM EASY TO CONSULT AND TRUST.

BASIC PERSONALITY

Taureans like to build themselves a home in which they can feel secure, and they prefer to work in a stable environment. Ruled by Venus, they have strong aesthetic tastes and like to create beautiful surroundings. They have methodical, decisive minds, but can be inflexible and reluctant to change.

Relationships Taureans are considerate lovers who enjoy sensual pleasure, but they can regard a lover as a possession, and jealousy can threaten the most secure partnership. Their ambition for a comfortable home can be so strong that they may neglect their partner and children in their eagerness to earn a sufficient income. Taurean children are usually happy and content, but need routine.

Career Taureans are ambitious but do not like risks – a regular income is very important to them. Their interest in money is not only emotional, but highly practical too. They are commonly found in careers connected with money such as banking and insurance. They also enjoy agriculture and horticulture, or any work that takes them out in the open air. Often interested in music, they make excellent musicians, especially singers.

Leisure Taureans enjoy their leisure and often pursue outdoor interests such as gardening or golf. They love food and wine but tend to put on weight. Aerobics, dancing, or jogging can help to keep the Taurean body trim.

Traditional Associations
Taurus is an earth sign and its ruling planet is Venus. It is a feminine sign and its symbol is the Bull.

Emerald
The emerald is a Taurean gemstone.

TAURUS AS ASCENDANT

If Taurus was rising at the moment of birth, there will be an almost irresistible need to acquire possessions – even stronger than if the Sun occupies the sign. People with Taurus rising like to be surrounded by the physical evidence of their success and status, and this can make them appear worldly and materialistic in their outlook on life. They are likely to have intense personal relationships, but possessiveness tends to be a problem.

TAURUS AS MIDHEAVEN

When the Midheaven falls in Taurus, Cancer, Leo, or Virgo will be in the Ascendant in northern latitudes, while in the southern hemisphere, Gemini, Cancer, or Leo will be rising. This Midheaven shows a need for emotional and financial security. Gemini rising means the subject's desires clash with Taurean needs, and conflict will arise between what is expected out of life and the means to achieve it. Security will be gained through shrewdness in business if Cancer is rising, while rigid determination will be directed towards aspirations when Leo rises. A practical approach to ambitions will be present when the Ascendant is Virgo.

Rose
The pink rose is often associated with Taurus.

Bull
Cattle traditionally come under the dominance of Taurus.

Taurus glyph

PLANETS
SUN
MOON
MERCURY
VENUS
MARS
JUPITER
SATURN
URANUS
NEPTUNE
PLUTO

SIGNS
ARIES
TAURUS
GEMINI
CANCER
LEO
VIRGO
LIBRA
SCORPIO
SAGITTARIUS
CAPRICORN
AQUARIUS
PISCES

THE SUN IN GEMINI

VERSATILE AND COMMUNICATIVE, GEMINIANS CAN ALSO BE SUPERFICIAL AND INCONSISTENT. THEY TEND TO BE WITTY AND LIVELY, AND REMAIN YOUTHFUL IN OLD AGE. GEMINIANS RARELY DO ONE THING AT A TIME – THEY WILL READ TWO BOOKS AT ONCE, WRITE LETTERS WHILE WATCHING TELEVISION, OR HOLD DOWN TWO JOBS.

BASIC PERSONALITY

Geminians have a talent for communication, and journalism is an ideal occupation for them. They tend to have very quick intellects fired by curiosity, and rational minds. Their strong sense of logic enables them to grasp the elements of a situation or subject quickly.

Relationships A dull partner, however attractive, will not be tolerated long by a Geminian. Shared interests are important but not necessarily shared views, because discussion and argument are the spice of life to a Gemini. Geminians make lively parents, but can be too fault-finding, forgetting that their child may not be so quick-minded as themselves. The Gemini child is intelligent, but is easily bored and should be encouraged to finish all tasks that are started.

Career Work in all branches of the media is ideal for communicative and versatile Geminians. They are often natural salespeople, and prove to be shrewd in business. However, they dislike solitary work and may be unhappy if they are promoted to lonely positions of power.

Leisure Geminians do not know what leisure is; they fill every moment with activity and are always seeking out ways to amuse themselves. They should burn off their nervous energy with sports such as squash, tennis, or jogging.

Traditional Associations
Gemini is an air sign and its ruling planet is Mercury. It is a masculine sign and its symbol is the Twins.

GEMINI AS ASCENDANT

If Gemini was rising at the moment of birth, the disposition to be ruled by logic will be strong. These people endlessly question themselves, their attitudes, and motives. In relationships, those with Gemini rising will insist that their partners fulfil themselves and achieve their ambitions, and intellectual compatibility will be a necessity. Friends are very important to them, and they will be reluctant to confine themselves within a relationship that denies them the freedom to have close friendships with others.

GEMINI AS MIDHEAVEN

When the Midheaven is Gemini, Leo or Virgo will be in the Ascendant in northern latitudes. In southern latitudes, Cancer, Leo, or Virgo will be rising. The desire to communicate will be important to those with Gemini Midheaven, and they will enjoy listening and taking part in debate. How the communication is expressed depends on the rising sign. Cancer rising can sometimes bestow literary talent if the birth chart shows creative potential. When Leo is rising, the individual may express opinions in a dogmatic way. A happy combination is Gemini Midheaven and Virgo rising, because both are ruled by Mercury. This union indicates an exceptional ability to communicate with other people.

Agate
The agate is a Geminian gemstone.

Lavender
Sweet-smelling lavender is associated with Gemini.

Gemini glyph

Parrot
Brightly coloured birds, such as the parrot, are ruled by Gemini.

THE SUN IN CANCER

EMOTIONAL, LOVING, AND PROTECTIVE, WITH A SHREWD BUT SOMETIMES MOODY
NATURE, CANCERIANS ARE HIGHLY DEFENSIVE, INTENT ON PROTECTING THEMSELVES
AND THOSE THEY LOVE FROM ATTACKS OF ANY KIND. EVEN A BREATH OF CRITICISM
WILL BE TAKEN PERSONALLY, AND THERE IS OFTEN A FIERCE RESPONSE.

BASIC PERSONALITY

Kindness and caring are strong
Cancerian characteristics, and
their instinct and intuition are
keen. If problems arise they
show natural courage and
resolution in adversity.

Relationships Cancerians are
naturally caring partners and
sensual lovers. They are firmly
committed to their partner and
family, and demand an equal
commitment in return. They
can be deeply sentimental, and
will be easily hurt and upset by
insensitivity. Cancerians cosset
their children, and suffer more
than usual when they grow
up and leave home. Even in
childhood, Cancerians are
intuitive and sensitive, which
may give rise to volatile moods.

Traditional Associations
Cancer is a water sign and its ruling
planet is the Moon. It is a feminine
sign and its symbol is the Crab.

CANCER AS ASCENDANT

Gemstone
The pearl is
a Cancerian
gemstone.

The caring
instinct is
particularly
strong when
Cancer is rising
at the moment of birth. The
homemaking impulse can
be very powerful in Cancer-
Ascendant people, and in a
partnership they are supportive
and ambitious for their lover.
Those without a family will
channel their homemaking
instincts into a worthy cause –
often charitable or ideological.
They often worry unnecessarily
about their health and this can
become a way of life.

Career All roles
in the caring
professions
attract Cancerians, while their
strong sense of nostalgia often
draws them to the antiques
business, or to work in
museums. They are
extremely canny and
this sign often confers
excellent commercial
sense. In business
their instinct and
intuition serve them
particularly well.

Lily
White flowers, such as
the lily, are associated
with Cancer.

CANCER AS MIDHEAVEN

When Cancer is
on the Midheaven in
northern and southern latitudes,
Libra or Scorpio will be in the
Ascendant. People with Cancer
as Midheaven will identify with
the family and home. They have a deep respect for
tradition, and do not find it easy to accept any form of
change. When Libra is rising, Libran indecision is likely
to be expressed through a desire to maintain the status
quo, but the relaxed, laid-back attitude should help to
combat the Cancerian tendency to worry. Scorpio and
Cancer are both water signs, therefore there is
little conflict if Scorpio is rising. The powerful,
emotionally charged motivation of Scorpio will
be a considerable advantage to the individual
when he or she tries to achieve
the ambitions of Cancer.

Crab
Cancer's
symbol is
the Crab.

Leisure Regular, rhythmical
exercise such as swimming and dancing is
recommended for Cancerians, who often have
delicate constitutions. The digestive system can
suffer from time to time, especially when the
individual is worried or over-stressed, and many
Cancerians are easily upset by changes of diet.

Cancer glyph

SUN
MOON
MERCURY
VENUS
MARS
JUPITER
SATURN
URANUS
NEPTUNE
PLUTO
SIGNS
ARIES
TAURUS
GEMINI
CANCER
LEO
VIRGO
LIBRA
SCORPIO
SAGITTARIUS
CAPRICORN
AQUARIUS
PISCES

Planets sidebar:
SUN · MOON · MERCURY · VENUS · MARS · JUPITER · SATURN · URANUS · NEPTUNE · PLUTO

SIGNS sidebar:
ARIES · TAURUS · GEMINI · CANCER · LEO · VIRGO · LIBRA · SCORPIO · SAGITTARIUS · CAPRICORN · AQUARIUS · PISCES

THE SUN IN LEO

GENEROUS, CREATIVE, AND ENTHUSIASTIC, LEO INDIVIDUALS ARE OFTEN AMONG THE MOST POPULAR MEMBERS OF SOCIETY, AND WITH THEIR NATURAL, LOVING FAITHFULNESS, AMONG THE MOST DESIRABLE OF PARTNERS. OCCASIONALLY THESE VIRTUES CAN LEAD TO POMPOSITY AND AN IMPERIOUS ATTITUDE TOWARDS OTHERS.

BASIC PERSONALITY

Leos have the strongest creative urge of all the Sun signs, and this must be expressed either practically, such as in gardening or dressmaking, or artistically, in painting, composing music, or writing. They are full of vitality, and any Leo unable to express his or her creativity will be frustrated and unhappy.

Relationships Leos can be surprisingly sensitive and easily hurt. Infidelity strikes not merely at their heart but at their sense of self-assurance. They are sensual and enjoy sex, but it must always be in comfortable surroundings. Adult Leos encourage talent in their children, but should beware of pushing them too hard. Leo children have sunny dispositions, but they like to organize, and parents should correct early signs of bossiness.

Traditional Associations
Leo is a fire sign and its ruling planet is the Sun. It is a masculine sign and its symbol is the Lion.

Ruby
The ruby is a Leo gemstone.

LEO AS ASCENDANT

When Leo is rising at the time of birth, organizational ability will be enhanced – but so will self-assurance, possibly even to the point of pride and vanity. Some individuals may find it difficult to see this fault in themselves. Creative instincts may be sacrificed because attention is given to the acquisition of wealth.

LEO AS MIDHEAVEN

When Leo is on the Midheaven in the northern hemisphere, Libra, Scorpio, or Sagittarius will be in the Ascendant. In the southern hemisphere, Scorpio, Sagittarius, or Capricorn will be rising. Leo Midheaven bestows a need to achieve and display the signs of success. People with Libra rising are unlikely to be outwardly ambitious, but will hope that the good things in life will simply fall into their laps. Sometimes they tend to be carried by others, using their Libran charm to achieve Leo objectives. When Scorpio rises, the determination and powerful energy of that sign, combined with Leo aspiration, offers these individuals everything that is necessary to make them extremely high achievers. However, care is needed if this powerful potential is to be fulfilled. Those with a Sagittarian Ascendant will be optimistic and enthusiastic for their ambitions. Driving ambition is present if Capricorn rises, and any power complexes must be controlled.

Career Intensely ambitious, Leos are interested in money for the comfort and beauty it can buy. They enjoy a sense of drama in their work, and a job in the theatre is a strong possibility, but so is any trade in which glamour and luxury play a part.

Leisure Leos have strong constitutions that stand up well to their frenetic lives. They enjoy exercise with an imaginative element and love rich food, but should eat sparingly.

Tiger
Big cats, such as tigers and lions, are associated with Leo.

Sunflower
The sign of Leo rules vibrant yellow flowers such as sunflowers and marigolds.

Leo glyph

THE SUN IN VIRGO

RELIABLE, DILIGENT, AND MODEST, VIRGOANS HAVE CONSIDERABLE NERVOUS ENERGY.
THIS CAN BE A SPLENDID ATTRIBUTE IF POSITIVELY USED, BUT IT CAN ALSO TURN
TO FUSSINESS AND OVER-FASTIDIOUSNESS IF UNCHECKED. VIRGOANS TEND TO
HAVE INNATE GOOD SENSE, AND THEIR ADVICE CAN BE TRUSTED.

BASIC PERSONALITY

Talkative, lively, and precise in conversation, Virgoans enjoy expressing themselves economically and clearly. Most of them are practical, but if they are not, they can be overwhelmed by fine detail and tend to over-analyze a situation.

Relationships Virgoans can be self-critical, and become convinced they are not good enough for their partner. This arises from a natural modesty that is otherwise attractive. Alternatively, they can be too critical of others – a trait that should be curbed. They work hard to provide for the family, but should be careful not to neglect their partner and offspring. Virgoan children may be naturally shy, and self-confidence should be encouraged by their parents.

Career Virgoans make first-rate personal assistants, and their critical sense can be a great help to colleagues less devoted to fine detail. They also make excellent teachers and doctors.

Leisure Fresh air is essential for Virgoans to enjoy good health. Holistic remedies often suit them, and if they find life is becoming frenetic, relaxation techniques such as yoga help to restore their equilibrium.

Traditional Associations
Virgo is an earth sign and is ruled by Mercury. It is a feminine sign and its symbol is the Virgin.

Primula
Small, brightly coloured flowers, such as primula, are associated with Virgo.

Rabbit
Virgo rules small animals such as rabbits.

Virgo glyph

VIRGO AS ASCENDANT

If Virgo is in the Ascendant at the time of birth, the subject will want to examine situations in detail, and communicate the results. The personality tends to be well integrated, but the Virgoan disposition to worry will be exacerbated. Self-praise should be encouraged. Finding the ideal partnership should not prove difficult, but these people do have a tendency to choose the easy option.

Sardonyx
The sardonyx is a Virgoan gemstone.

VIRGO AS MIDHEAVEN

When the sign of Virgo is on the Midheaven in northern latitudes, Scorpio will be in the Ascendant. In southern latitudes, either Sagittarius or Capricorn will be rising. A Virgo Midheaven reveals a need to communicate. The sleuth-like qualities present when Scorpio rises ensure that the individual will leave no stone unturned in his or her pursuit of ambitions and objectives. This is an ideal combination for those who choose a Virgoan profession such as research, detection, or medicine. When Sagittarius is rising, an identification with Virgoan love of detail often clashes with Sagittarian breadth of vision, but if individuals can combine Virgoan caution with their optimistic attitude to life they should eventually find success. A Capricorn Ascendant will add a practical and common-sense attitude to the subject, because both Virgo and Capricorn are earth signs.

PLANETS

SUN
MOON
MERCURY
VENUS
MARS
JUPITER
SATURN
URANUS
NEPTUNE
PLUTO

SIGNS

ARIES
TAURUS
GEMINI
CANCER
LEO
VIRGO
LIBRA
SCORPIO
SAGITTARIUS
CAPRICORN
AQUARIUS
PISCES

PLANETS

SUN

MOON

MERCURY

VENUS

MARS

JUPITER

SIGNS

ARIES

TAURUS

GEMINI

CANCER

LEO

VIRGO

LIBRA

SCORPIO

SAGITTARIUS

CAPRICORN

AQUARIUS

PISCES

THE SUN IN LIBRA

DIPLOMATIC, ROMANTIC, AND IDEALISTIC, LIBRANS NEED BALANCE FOR A HARMONIOUS LIFE. IN ORDER TO ATTAIN THIS STATE OF EQUILIBRIUM, THEY WILL SOMETIMES GIVE WAY IN SITUATIONS WHERE THEY SHOULD STAND FIRM, OR SIT ON THE FENCE UNTIL SOMEONE ELSE HAS RESOLVED THE PROBLEM, OR IT HAS SIMPLY RESOLVED ITSELF.

BASIC PERSONALITY

Procrastination comes naturally to Librans, because they have the ability to see every point of view, and dislike taking sides in an argument. Although they have considerable physical energy, they are sometimes accused of laziness. This is often because they are choosing to relax, and making time to listen to the problems of their friends and family.

Relationships Librans are great romantics, and they are vulnerable when in a partnership. The usual Libran indecision is swept aside, and when marrying in haste they may repent at leisure. Libran parents are very loving and caring, but sometimes spoil their children for the sake of peace and quiet. Libran children are easy to please, and tend to rely on a parent to make decisions.

Snake
Small reptiles and snakes are ruled by Libra.

Career Librans enjoy the high life, and need to earn good money. They thrive in positions that need diplomacy and tact; fashion, and the beauty and cosmetic industries suit them well.

Leisure Librans do not enjoy physical exertion, but they need to exercise to avoid becoming overweight. They should also control their love of rich food.

Traditional Associations
Libra is an air sign and its ruling planet is Venus. It is a masculine sign and its symbol is the Scales.

Hydrangeas
Most blue flowers, including hydrangeas, come under the dominion of Libra.

Libra glyph

Sapphire
The sapphire is a Libran gemstone.

LIBRA AS ASCENDANT

The effect of Libra is not especially strong when it is rising at the moment of birth, but it will endow the subject with some Libran characteristics. These include the need to relate to a partner, and an exacerbation of any tendency to rush into love affairs, or even a permanent relationship. It will bring with it sensuality and a greater enthusiasm for sex than is often the case with a Libran person. The Libran influence can make the subject self-satisfied, disinclined to self-criticism, and likely to use considerable charm to disguise personal flaws. Self-analysis is useful to these people, who should be encouraged to know and understand themselves.

LIBRA AS MIDHEAVEN

When the sign of Libra is on the Midheaven in northern latitudes, either Sagittarius or Capricorn will be in the Ascendant. In southern latitudes, Capricorn or Aquarius will be rising. In general, these individuals will identify with a peaceful existence, even if this is not part of their daily reality. The Libran liking for comfort can weaken the more devil-may-care motivation of Sagittarius, while if Capricorn is rising, a prim and proper attitude to life can give way to Libran easy-living when temptation arises. The combination of Libra and Aquarius causes the subject to aspire to individuality, but without the motivation to do anything about it.

THE SUN IN SCORPIO

PASSIONATE AND FORCEFUL, INTUITIVE AND MAGNETIC, SCORPIOS ARE ALSO LIKELY TO BE JEALOUS AND OBSTINATE. JEALOUSY IS INDEED THEIR WORST FAULT – JEALOUSY OF A PARTNER, A COLLEAGUE, EVEN OF A NEIGHBOUR'S POSSESSIONS. THE HIDDEN BENEFIT IS THAT SCORPIOS WILL WORK HARD TO ATTAIN THE OBJECT OF THEIR JEALOUSY.

BASIC PERSONALITY

Scorpios are regularly accused of being obsessively interested in sex. This allegation arises simply from the fact that Scorpio rules the genitals. Many Scorpios express their sexual energy through sport and work. It is vital to them that their abundant energy is positively used. Scorpios are capable of very deep and systematic thought, and can get to the root of any problem.

Relationships

Energetic Scorpios need a sympathetic partner who will meet their physical and emotional demands with empathy and warmth. Finding such a person, they will pursue him or her with the utmost intensity. Scorpios demand a great deal of their children and are eager for them to be successful. Scorpio children tend to bottle up their emotions and should be encouraged to communicate.

Traditional Associations
Scorpio is a water sign and its ruler is
Pluto. It is a feminine sign and its
symbol is the Scorpion.

Opal
The opal is
a Scorpio
gemstone.

SCORPIO AS ASCENDANT

Scorpio Sun-sign characteristics are more powerfully expressed when it is the rising sign. The tendency for these people to be secretive can become obsessive. Sometimes preoccupied with their faults, those who have Scorpio rising should give themselves credit for their virtues. Emotional security is important to them.

Insects
Scorpio
is linked
with
insects and
crustaceans.

Career Scorpios are very ambitious and can appear devoted to making money. Their sense of purpose means that they are often excellent business people, and their incisive minds help them to be successful researchers and detectives. They often become extremely involved in their work.

SCORPIO AS MIDHEAVEN

When Scorpio is on the Midheaven in northern latitudes, Capricorn or Aquarius will be in the Ascendant. In southern latitudes, Capricorn, Aquarius, or Pisces will be ascending. Identification with Scorpio interests and powerful motivation are important to those with this Midheaven, but their success depends on their rising and Sun signs. Capricorn rising can bring political aspirations, and fares better than Aquarius, whose unpredictable behaviour will have to be overcome before success can be assured. The Scorpio influence adds a sense of direction to those with Pisces rising.

Leisure Scorpios often wait until retirement before they take up any interest outside work. They are intense in work and play – moderation does not come easily, but should be cultivated. Swimming is especially good exercise for them, and they are attracted to the martial arts, for the physical aspects as well as the philosophy.

Geraniums
Red flowers, such
as geraniums, are
ruled by Scorpio.

Scorpio glyph

	PLANETS
☉	SUN
☽	MOON
☿	MERCURY
♀	VENUS
♂	MARS
♃	JUPITER
♄	SATURN
♅	URANUS
♆	NEPTUNE
♇	PLUTO

	SIGNS
♈	ARIES
♉	TAURUS
	CANCER
♌	LEO
♏	SCORPIO
♐	SAGITTARIUS
♑	CAPRICORN
♒	AQUARIUS
♓	PISCES

PLANETS

☉ SUN

☽ MOON

☿ MERCURY

♀ VENUS

♂ MARS

♃ JUPITER

♄ SATURN

♅ URANUS

♆ NEPTUNE

♇ PLUTO

SIGNS

♈ ARIES

♉ TAURUS

♊ GEMINI

♋ CANCER

♌ LEO

♍ VIRGO

♎ LIBRA

♐ SAGITTARIUS

♑

♒

♓

THE SUN IN SAGITTARIUS

OPTIMISTIC, GOOD-HUMOURED, AND FREEDOM-LOVING, SAGITTARIANS CAN BE OVER-EXUBERANT AND OCCASIONALLY TACTLESS. CHALLENGE IS IMPORTANT TO THEM, AND THEY ARE FOREVER SETTING NEW TARGETS FOR THEMSELVES. THEIR ENTHUSIASM IS ENVIABLY FORCEFUL, BUT RESTLESSNESS CAN BE A DIFFICULTY.

BASIC PERSONALITY

Sagittarians' enthusiasm can often lead to risk-taking and foolhardiness. They will need to govern, if not curb, their ardour. The Sagittarian tendency to move swiftly from one task to another is a useful quality, but there can be a tendency to do too many things at the same time. They have great breadth of vision but often find details boring.

Relationships Claustrophobia is the enemy of Sagittarians, and any partnership in which the lover is possessive will be difficult. Relationships need to be based on shared intellectual pursuits. Sagittarians make wonderful parents because they encourage and stimulate their children. Sagittarian children are enthusiastic and should be encouraged to concentrate their zeal in one direction.

Career Challenge is essential where a career is concerned; publishing and the law are typical Sagittarian professions. They tend to learn languages easily, and make enthusiastic teachers and lecturers.

Leisure Sagittarians enjoy physical and intellectual travel. They love food and drink, and even with a strict exercise regime tend to put on weight.

Traditional Associations
Sagittarius is a fire sign and is ruled by Jupiter. It is a masculine sign and its symbol is the Centaur.

Topaz
The topaz is a Sagittarian gemstone.

SAGITTARIUS AS ASCENDANT

The need for challenge is paramount when Sagittarius was rising at the moment of birth. Life without personal goals can seem rather meaningless to these people, and they may succumb to depression. Early encouragement will give them a head start, and great expectations should become superb achievements. They must allow plenty of time for thought – resolving problems without proper consideration can be seriously damaging. Friendship and intellectual rapport, as well as sexual compatibility, are necessary within a personal relationship.

SAGITTARIUS AS MIDHEAVEN

When Sagittarius is on the Midheaven in northern latitudes, Capricorn, Aquarius, or Pisces is in the Ascendant. In southern latitudes, Aquarius or Pisces is ascending. This Midheaven sign brings a desire for mental stimulation and a love of philosophy. Capricorn rising can lead to a conflict between conventionality and the desire to be adventurous. The Aquarian need for independence will combine well with a freedom of spirit that is essentially Sagittarian. Pisces rising can bring too much versatility, and in spite of high aspirations, there need to be signs of determination elsewhere in the birth chart.

Horse and Polo Player
Horses, and all animals associated with hunting, are ruled by Sagittarius.

Carnations
Sagittarius is associated with carnations.

Sagittarius glyph

THE SUN IN CAPRICORN

PRACTICAL AND PRUDENT, AMBITIOUS AND DISCIPLINED, CAPRICORNS CAN SEEM
CONVENTIONAL AND RIGID IN THEIR VIEWS. THEY ARE OFTEN THOUGHT TO BE
MISERLY AND GRUDGING, BOTH FINANCIALLY AND EMOTIONALLY, BUT IT IS OFTEN
A LACK OF SELF-CONFIDENCE THAT CAUSES CAPRICORNS TO BE SO INHIBITED.

BASIC PERSONALITY

Capricorns can be slaves to convention, always concerned to be seen to do the right thing. What often saves them is a captivating sense of humour, which can take over even at the most serious moments, disarming anyone who is about to give up on them. If a Capricorn can be persuaded to relax and break out in some way, a lighter side of his or her personality will emerge.

Relationships Capricorns find it difficult to express themselves verbally, and tend to regard their partners as possessions. They are always eager for the success of their children, but may place more emphasis on material wealth than love. Capricorn children are loyal, but need to be able to respect their parents, and have a secure environment.

Career

Capricorns relish working alone and exercising control – the self-made business person is often a Capricorn. If they do work with others, their ambition drives them steadily to the top of their career. They do well in local government, banking, and finance.

Leisure Outdoor activities such as gardening, golf, and walking will be enjoyed by Capricorns, but music and books give them great satisfaction too. Capricorns are more likely than most people to spend hours behind a desk, and exercise is necessary if they are not to develop stiffness in their joints and, at worst, arthritis.

Traditional Associations
Capricorn is an earth sign and its ruler is Saturn. It is a feminine sign and its symbol is the Goat.

Goat
All cloven-hoofed animals are ruled by Capricorn.

Amethyst
The amethyst is a Capricorn gemstone.

CAPRICORN AS ASCENDANT

The self-confidence of those born with Capricorn rising fluctuates badly, leaving them very unsure of themselves. They should learn to take themselves at others' high valuation. They show their emotion more easily than Sun-sign Capricorns, and will be more caring and sensitive to their partner's needs.

CAPRICORN AS MIDHEAVEN

When Capricorn is on the Midheaven in northern and southern latitudes, Aries or Taurus is in the Ascendant. Aries rising will identify completely with Capricorn ambition, and there will be a tendency to concentrate solely on material progress. These people may eventually occupy a lonely top position. When Taurus rises, the outlook is more conventional and practical. This group hates to step out of line, and while material progress will be extremely important, the Taurean need for security will be spiced with a Capricornian fancy for upward mobility and social climbing.

Capricorn glyph

Pansies
Amaranthus, heartsease, and pansies are associated with Capricorn.

PLANETS

SUN
MOON
MERCURY
VENUS
MARS
JUPITER
SATURN
URANUS
NEPTUNE
PLUTO
SIGNS
ARIES
TAURUS

VIRGO
LIBRA

SCORPIO
SAGITTARIUS

CAPRICORN
AQUARIUS

PISCES

PLANETS

☉
SUN

☽
MOON

☿
MERCURY

♀
VENUS

♂
MARS

♃
JUPITER

♄
SATURN

♅
URANUS

♆
NEPTUNE

♇
PLUTO

SIGNS

♈
ARIES

♉
TAURUS

♊
GEMINI

♋

♍
VIRGO

♎
LIBRA

♏
SCORPIO

♐
SAGITTARIUS

♑
CAPRICORN

♒
AQUARIUS

♓
PISCES

THE SUN IN AQUARIUS

ORIGINAL, INVENTIVE, HONEST, AND LOYAL, THE TYPICAL AQUARIAN MAY ALSO SEEM CONTRARY AND PERVERSE, AND WILL CERTAINLY BE UNPREDICTABLE. AQUARIANS NEED THEIR INDEPENDENCE AND PRIVACY. IT IS POSSIBLE TO BE THEIR LIFELONG FRIEND, YET FEEL THAT THEY HAVE ONLY EVER REVEALED THE SURFACE OF THEIR PERSONALITY.

BASIC PERSONALITY

Aquarians are likeable and open, and are always ready to be supportive to their friends. Highly conscious of the needs of others, they will help whenever they can. They need to express their originality in order to feel fulfilled.

Relationships Aquarians often find it difficult to sustain a close emotional relationship, because this means adjusting their lifestyle to accommodate the habits of another. When they make a commitment, they are extremely loyal, but they are likely to prevaricate before making any pledge. Aquarian parents often find it difficult to understand a child who is more conventional than themselves, while an Aquarian child's individuality is sometimes construed as waywardness.

Traditional Associations
Aquarius is an air sign and is ruled by the planet Uranus. It is a masculine sign and its symbol is the Water Carrier.

Aquamarine
An Aquarian gemstone is the aquamarine.

AQUARIUS AS ASCENDANT

When Aquarius is the sign rising at the time of birth, the craving for independence is even more acute than for Sun-sign Aquarians, and the individual may have a distant air that makes it difficult to know him or her. The best quality of these Aquarians is their desire, even need, to help others. Properly employed, this characteristic can make it somewhat easier for them to open up and allow others to support them. Stubbornness and personal rigidity can be a considerable problem when Aquarius is the Ascendant.

AQUARIUS AS MIDHEAVEN

When Aquarius is on the Midheaven in northern latitudes, Taurus, Gemini, or Cancer is in the Ascendant. In southern latitudes, Aries, Taurus, or Gemini will be ascending. The Aquarian Midheaven adds individuality, especially when Aries is the rising sign. When the fixed sign Taurus is present, the desire for individualism can conflict with the conventional qualities of that sign, and stubbornness and eccentricity may result. Gemini rising bestows an original mind. In all cases there will be an interest in humanitarian causes, but especially when Cancer rises; the caring qualities combine in an individual who takes positive action to help other people.

Orchid
The many flowers ruled by Aquarius include the orchid.

Career Aquarians enjoy work in humanitarian professions and in communications, such as the technical areas of television and radio. Their natural sense of drama often finds expression in theatre work, the fashion industry, and in careers that call for flair and originality.

Leisure Aquarians possess originality and creativity, and should try to express these qualities in their leisure activities. Regular, creative exercise, such as dancing, is most beneficial for them. However, the ankles are ruled by this sign and can be vulnerable, so care should be taken to protect them, especially if skiing or winter sports are enjoyed. Like all air-sign people, Aquarians thrive best on a light, nourishing diet.

Aquarius glyph

Goose Feathers
Large, far-flying birds, such as geese, are ruled by Aquarius.

THE SUN IN PISCES

IMAGINATIVE AND IDEALISTIC, PISCEANS CAN BE A LITTLE TOO UNWORLDLY, AND THE SYMBOL OF THE SIGN – TWO FISHES SWIMMING IN OPPOSITE DIRECTIONS – REFLECTS THEIR TENDENCY TO SELF-DECEPTION, TO FACE BOTH WAYS AT ONCE. HOWEVER, PISCES IS ABOVE ALL THE CREATIVE SIGN OF THE DREAMER AND THE POET.

BASIC PERSONALITY

Pisceans are among the most compassionate and kindly of people, often giving more time to the problems of others than they allow for consideration of their own. Their imagination, positively expressed, is an enormous asset, but Pisceans must learn not to allow their imagination to work negatively, magnifying small problems into major ones. They also tend to lie to themselves and others, rather than face harsh reality.

Relationships Sensitive and romantic, Pisceans often seem ready to deceive themselves rather than to admit any fault in their beloved. They are not especially passionate; their view of sex is essentially a romantic one. As parents, Pisceans are very encouraging to their children, but can be too easy-going. Piscean children tend to embroider the truth, and are better taught to be honest from an early age. They should be encouraged to use their strong imaginations positively.

Traditional Associations
Pisces is a water sign and is ruled by the planet Neptune. It is a water sign and its symbol is two Fishes.

Fish
Water-loving mammals, and fish, are ruled by Pisces.

Career Pisceans have an innate talent for caring and are always ready to listen to other people, so they can make exceptional counsellors. They love beauty, and will work contentedly in any area of the arts.

Leisure Highly sensitive to atmosphere, Pisceans' constitutions are easily disturbed by tension, and stress can cause them to over-eat or drink. Tension should be relieved with inspirational exercise such as yoga or t'ai chi.

Pisces glyph

PISCES AS ASCENDANT

People born while Pisces is rising can fit into any environment, but they tend to become so much part of their surroundings that others take them for granted. However, their work behind the scenes will be unremitting and valuable. Self-knowledge is difficult for them, and they may even invent a persona and shape themselves to it, rather than seek out their own true personality. They tend to be hypochondriacs, and can be critical of their partners.

Moonstone
A Piscean gemstone is the moonstone.

PISCES ON MIDHEAVEN

When Pisces is on the Midheaven in northern latitudes, Gemini or Cancer is in the Ascendant. In southern latitudes, Taurus or Gemini will be ascending. These individuals will aspire to be kind, gentle, and flexible, but their level of success depends on their rising sign. When Taurus is the Ascendant, there is common sense and a practical approach to life, which will quell the Piscean tendency to evade reality. People with Gemini rising will be in tune with the secretive and deceitful qualities of Pisces, and these clever, quick thinkers will sometimes enjoy scheming and being deliberately deceptive. There may be an identification with a religious faith, or some kind of spiritual path for those with Cancer rising.

Viburnum
All types of green flowers, such as viburnum, are associated with Pisces.

PLANETS	
	SUN
	MOON
	MERCURY
	VENUS
	MARS
	JUPITER
	SATURN
	URANUS
	NEPTUNE
	PLUTO

SIGNS	
	ARIES
	TAURUS
	GEMINI
	CANCER
	LEO
	VIRGO
	LIBRA
	SCORPIO
	SAGITTARIUS
	CAPRICORN
	AQUARIUS
	PISCES

PLANETS

☉ SUN

☽ MOON

☿ MERCURY

♀ VENUS

♂ MARS

♃ JUPITER

♄ SATURN

♅ URANUS

♆ NEPTUNE

♇ PLUTO

SIGNS

♈ ARIES

♉ TAURUS

♊ GEMINI

♋ CANCER

♌ LEO

♍ VIRGO

♎ LIBRA

♏ SCORPIO

♐ SAGITTARIUS

♑ CAPRICORN

♒ AQUARIUS

♓ PISCES

THE MOON THROUGH THE SIGNS

The sign in which the Moon falls at our birth reflects the way we respond emotionally and intuitively to situations, and our attitudes to aspects of everyday life. The position of the Moon will also indicate which elements of our personalities we inherit from our parents and ancestors. Inherited characteristics may be resisted by us but they are nonetheless powerful, and understanding our emotional reactions can contribute to our psychological development. The Moon's activities are strengthened by positive aspects between it and the Sun or the chart's ruling planet, the Ascendant's ruler.

♈ THE MOON IN ARIES

THOSE WITH THE Moon in Aries at the time of their birth react immediately and very passionately to situations in which they are emotionally involved, and sometimes the response can be rather too hasty. An instinctive need for action sometimes results in rash decision-making. This can be dangerous in situations where carelessness can lead to injury – for instance in sports such as rock-climbing or motor-racing. Where everyday life is concerned, Aries Moon people should learn to be patient with those slower than themselves. A quick emotional reaction is not always advisable, and they should cultivate control and resist temptation towards aggression or confrontation. However, if the Moon receives negative aspects from Mars or Uranus, the tendency towards a quick temper may be irresistible.

The positive aspect of the Moon in Aries is that these people are decisive when others are confused, and have a broad grasp of most situations. They need independence and are quick to encourage others to be independent too. Easily bored, they need innovation in all areas of their lives. The Arien tendency towards selfishness is certainly not lacking, and in personal matters they tend to put themselves first – but they are quick to acknowledge when they have been selfish.

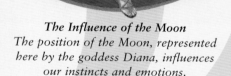

The Influence of the Moon
The position of the Moon, represented here by the goddess Diana, influences our instincts and emotions.

♉ THE MOON IN TAURUS

TRADITIONALLY, the Moon is exalted in Taurus, making its influence especially powerful. Those people born with the Moon in this sign are protective of their physical and emotional environment, and tend to respond defensively when their security is under threat. Even if they do not seem concerned about their income, or their partner's happiness, they will be quick to act when anything may affect them. These people tend to be obsessed with themselves and their own problems, and to some extent share Taurus conventionality and fixation on doing the right thing. This may conflict with other areas of the

birth chart – but if there is a Capricorn Sun or Ascendant, the tendency will be less likely to cause a clash within the personality. There will be a strong element of practicality and common sense, but problems may arise because of the Taurean tendency to be possessive and stubborn, exacerbated if fixed signs are emphasized in the birth chart. The Taurean love of good food and good living can be very strong when the Moon is in this sign. Unfortunately, Taureans tend to put on weight easily, and will need to resist over-consumption of rich food if their figure, and their digestion, are not to suffer.

♊ THE MOON IN GEMINI

VERSATILITY IS LIKELY to be shown by people with their Moon in Gemini. They tend to read more than one book at a time, and never perform one task without trying at the same time to cope with another. This tendency may arise in relationships, and an emotional involvement with more than one person at a time is common; it will not, however, necessarily become a physical involvement. The first reaction of these people is likely to be a verbal one – often so rapidly expressed that it is incoherent. They are logical and rational, and there may be a conflict in their personality if other areas of the horoscope encourage them to be emotional and intuitive. People with a Gemini Moon need to understand these conflicting elements and to learn that the contrasting traits can complement each other. Logic can be tempered by intuition, and vice versa.

Impatience and restlessness may be felt and there will be a great deal of nervous energy that will need positive expression. Nervous strain can sometimes lead to tension and digestive problems. Asthma could perhaps be inherent, which may be another result of undue tension. Positive aspects between the Moon and other personal planets will help to stabilize the personality.

THE MOON IN CANCER

THE MOON RULES Cancer, therefore its position in this sign at the time of birth is particularly influential. People with this placing will be defensive and protective of their environment, even in everyday circumstances. Intuition is likely to be especially strong and reliable, though it is useful if elsewhere in the horoscope there are indications of more down-to-earth characteristics. For example, the Sun or Mercury in an earth sign, or a trine aspect to Saturn from the Moon itself, will keep intuition and emotion under control. A committed relationship is necessary for these people's well-being, but they tend to have mood swings that are difficult for partners to deal with. Their homes may be cluttered because nostalgia prevents them from throwing things away.

The family is very important to those with their Moon in Cancer and their tendency to worry about the well-being of loved ones can take on unwarranted proportions. They make excellent parents, but need to control the urge to be overprotective towards their offspring if they are not to drive them away. Anxiety upsets their digestive system, and often they have very sensitive skin that should not be exposed to strong sunlight.

THE MOON IN LEO

THIS POSITION IS often found in the birth chart of high achievers, especially if the Moon is near the Midheaven, or placed in the tenth house. People with their Moon in Leo can appear overbearing and dogmatic: their immediate instinct in almost any situation is to take over. They are self-centred, and this can lead to arrogance and stubbornness. On the other hand, they usually have the best of motives, and can be a source of inspiration to others. They will find every possible outlet for their potential (which will be indicated by the characteristics of the Sun sign) and will achieve their personal aspirations. They rarely do this, however, without going a little too far in the eyes of partners, friends, or colleagues. There is an unconscious need for admiration and attention from others, and if shyness or inhibition is indicated elsewhere in the horoscope, the conflict will result in a tendency to show off and appear over-confident. They cope well in emergencies, for the qualities of leadership inherent in Leo will always be present.

This is a placing that needs a steadying influence from other planets in the birth chart. Children with their Moon in this sign can be excessively exuberant, and they should be encouraged to control this trait before it develops into bombast.

THE MOON IN VIRGO

ENORMOUS RESERVES of nervous energy are offered by this position of the Moon, as well as a great deal of common sense and reliability. There will also be practical skill, and an ability to think quickly and respond swiftly to situations. They tend to be perfectionists who appear capable and confident to others, but true self-confidence may be lacking. They would prefer to work behind the scenes, and do not like to draw attention to themselves. They also

The Moon in Tarot
This Italian tarot card dates from 1896. It depicts a Full Moon, when its influence is considered most powerful.

respect the privacy of others, and rarely ask personal questions unless they relate to their work. There will be a tendency to worry, which is often at the root of the digestive problems or mysterious stomach complaints that tend to afflict these subjects at times of tension. The intuitive influence of the Moon does not always combine well with the rationality of Virgo. They can become over-obsessive about the most inconsequential details, and fail to see the broader issue. These people have a critical streak and, if the Moon receives a square aspect from Mercury, a tendency to gossip. Interested and knowledgeable about health and hygiene, cleanliness is very important to them. They are talented and incisive in debate, though susceptible to being over-talkative when nervous. While not openly competitive, they like to keep abreast of competitors, and often have no difficulty outstripping them.

PLANETS

SUN

MOON

MERCURY

VENUS

MARS

JUPITER

SATURN

URANUS

NEPTUNE

PLUTO

SIGNS

ARIES

TAURUS

GEMINI

CANCER

LEO

VIRGO

LIBRA

SCORPIO

SAGITTARIUS

CAPRICORN

AQUARIUS

PISCES

PLANETS

SUN

MOON

MERCURY

VENUS

MARS

ARIES

TAURUS

GEMINI

CANCER

LEO

VIRGO

LIBRA

SCORPIO

SAGITTARIUS

CAPRICORN

AQUARIUS

PISCES

♎ THE MOON IN LIBRA

ANYONE BORN WHEN the Moon was in Libra will have the ability to be a peacemaker. Tactful, sympathetic, and also naturally diplomatic and understanding, they are able to identify freely with other people and their points of view. Meeting these people, we immediately feel at ease, and may well envy their relaxed air. They have a direct, beguiling charm,

Moon Calendar
This hand-painted Breton calendar dating from 1546 depicts the cycles of the Moon.

and an engaging way of talking that is instantly attractive. These people will be of the greatest help in a crisis. Naturally calm, they remain above the fray, able to see situations clearly and completely. The only drawback to this placing is that it can lead to indecision, and at worst weaken the character so that these subjects find it extremely difficult to resolve personal difficulties. Look for emphasis on the stronger signs in the horoscope – Capricorn or Leo, for instance – to counter this possible debility. Libra's opposite sign is Aries, and if this sign features in the chart it may encourage a slightly aggressive tendency that can sometimes provoke the starting of an argument when one is not strictly necessary. The typical Libran cry of "but it isn't fair!" will be heard occasionally. Libran balance and harmony are qualities that will be

present in these characters, and will be useful at times of tension, when they can restore harmony with partners, friends, or colleagues.

♏ THE MOON IN SCORPIO

THE EMOTIONS of people with this placing of the Moon are particularly strong and easily tapped. Emotion is forceful in anyone who has a strong emphasis on Scorpio in their birth chart (perhaps as Sun sign or Ascendant); in this case it is even more potent, and will surface immediately when the individual feels challenged. Almost any situation can give rise to an emotional outburst, and stubbornness and wilful behaviour are common in these people. They are likely to take a very strong line with anyone who dares to oppose them and there will also be an inclination towards jealousy. They have the potential to brood over any slight, and can bear a grudge over a long period. They may even plan revenge and wait patiently for the opportune moment. Awareness of these traits may enable these individuals to curb them, but their desires are so strongly linked to their emotions that they often have difficulty in being objective. It is important to express positively the considerable emotion channelled by this placing of the Moon; negative expression of such powerful feeling can endanger the psychological balance. Physical energy and the strong determination to succeed are also boosted, and, if motivation is directed in a positive way, almost any aspiration or goal can be achieved.

♐ THE MOON IN SAGITTARIUS

THIS POSITION of the Moon offers optimism and a positive outlook – but it is possible that over-optimism and a tendency to react too swiftly

and move on too rapidly may cloud the judgement, unless there are other more sobering influences to be found elsewhere in the birth chart. Nevertheless, this is quite a favourable position for the Moon, which will impart much of the natural Sagittarian positive attitude to challenge. These people enjoy having their intellects stretched and like to test themselves in difficult circumstances, relishing any trial of their abilities, but they can sometimes give the impression of knowing and understanding much more than is really the case. Hope and optimism run high, but there is also a tendency to be off-hand because the attention has already moved on to another subject.

There is often a lack of attention to detail, and Sagittarian restlessness and impatience, combined with the urge to move forward, can lead to the relinquishing of a task before it has been properly completed. Indeed, these subjects are often bad drivers, lane-hopping and horn-blowing when delayed by other cars. There is great intellectual potential, but these subjects need to learn to apply themselves consistently and to complete their tasks thoroughly. Sun-sign Sagittarians are philosophically inclined, and those with their Moon in Sagittarius should cultivate a philosophical frame of mind, and try to quell their over-enthusiasm. They need to learn to recognize and appreciate the details of a situation, while retaining the Sagittarian ability to see the overall picture.

♑ THE MOON IN CAPRICORN

WHEN THE MOON shines from Capricorn, it sheds a somewhat cool light on the personality; emotion can be cold and self-control is strong. They appear aloof and tend to consider themselves superior to the rest of humanity. This rather unendearing attitude is occasionally alleviated by the typical off-beat Capricorn sense of humour, which they often use to soften their

PLANETS

☉ SUN

☽ MOON

☿ MERCURY

♀ VENUS

♂ MARS

♃ JUPITER

♄ SATURN

♅ URANUS

♆ NEPTUNE

♇ PLUTO

SIGNS

♈ ARIES

♉ TAURUS

♊ GEMINI

♋ CANCER

♌ LEO

♍ VIRGO

♎ LIBRA

♏ SCORPIO

♐ SAGITTARIUS

♑ CAPRICORN

♒ AQUARIUS

♓ PISCES

compulsive need to complain about everything. They are often moody, and their initial response to a situation tends to be negative, especially if the Moon makes a square or opposition aspect to Saturn. They avoid excitement or challenge, and possess a powerful sense of self-preservation, so that only calculated risks will be taken.

These subjects set their sights on success, and are intent on fulfilling their ambitions; with encouragement from planets well placed elsewhere in the chart, they will probably do so. They will be eager to achieve their goals without the help of others: they have a strong sense of pride and tend to reject assistance, however well meant. Self-satisfaction may show itself in the desire to impress other people with the trappings of success. They are materialistic, and have a very strong need for financial security and status. If the Moon is well aspected – especially if there is a trine to Mars, Saturn, the Ascendant, or Sun – this placing is much more beneficial, enabling these subjects to use the strong, practical aspects of their characters quickly and decisively, but at the same time subduing Capricorn seriousness and encouraging them to enjoy life.

♒ THE MOON IN AQUARIUS

PEOPLE WITH THE Moon in Aquarius at birth can seem as cool as those with the planet in Capricorn – but these people are aloof rather than emotionally cold. They like to keep their distance, but a desire to comfort, reassure, and assist anyone who needs help will immediately dispel the coolness, and great practicality will be shown in resolving problems. It may take some time to get to know these subjects – indeed, it is doubtful whether anyone ever truly gets to

know them – but with patience it is possible to break down the barrier, and then the characteristics of their Sun or Ascendant sign will come through. They can be surprisingly romantic but to judge how they will react when in love it is best to look at the positions of Venus and Mars in their birth chart. Highly original characters, their reactions, especially in controversial situations, are often idiosyncratic, unconventional, and quite different from what might be anticipated. They are capable of acting on the spur of the moment, and completely out of character, and then having difficulty in justifying the

Cancer's Ruling Planet
The Moon rules the sign of Cancer, and those people born with a Cancer Sun sign display the intuition and emotional nature associated with the Moon.

action even to themselves. Nervous tension can be a problem for people with their Moon in Aquarius, and stubbornness, if it is indicated elsewhere in the birth chart, can be disastrous when combined with unpredictability. There is often originality and even a touch of genius in these subjects, and their bright ideas should never be rejected just because they seem unusual or irrational. Acted upon, they often turn out to be successful.

♓ THE MOON IN PISCES

TWO HIGHLY CHARGED FORCES meet when the Moon is in Pisces: the emotional force of the planet, and the emotional content of the sign. These individuals will be easily moved to happiness or sadness by music, literature, and art, and human tragedy affects them deeply. They give generously to appeals for money, sometimes to the point of self-denial. If the individual has a sense of vocation, this placing of the Moon, with its emphasis on positive, caring, sacrificial characteristics, will contribute strongly. There will be a powerful, natural empathy with other people who are suffering, and a very special sympathy with and understanding of those who need help. Their heightened emotional nature allows them to pick up unconsciously the feelings of others, and they can be affected by other people's moods. The Moon in Pisces is valuable to individuals who have creative elements elsewhere in their charts, because it aids their imagination and helps them to express their creativity. In the practical areas of life, the Pisces Moon may weaken the character – subjects will be inclined to take the line of least resistance, especially when challenged, and will not be good at standing up for their own ideas. There may be a tendency to be equivocal and deceptive, lying not only to other people but also to themselves. Like people who have a Piscean Sun sign or Ascendant, they may seek out some form of escapism, but they should avoid "recreational drugs", including tobacco and alcohol, because they can quickly become addicted.

Moon glyph

PLANETS

☉ SUN

☽ MOON

☿ MERCURY

♀ VENUS

♂ MARS

♃ JUPITER

♄ SATURN

♅ URANUS

♆ NEPTUNE

♇ PLUTO

SIGNS

♈ ARIES

♉ TAURUS

♊ GEMINI

♋ CANCER

♌ LEO

♍ VIRGO

♎ LIBRA

♏ SCORPIO

♐ SAGITTARIUS

♑ CAPRICORN

♒ AQUARIUS

♓ PISCES

MERCURY THROUGH THE SIGNS

Mercury's area of influence is the mind. From its placing in a birth chart we can form a picture of the way our minds work, whether we think logically or intuitively, and also how we communicate with others. Seen from the Earth, Mercury always appears close to the Sun. For astrological purposes, Mercury cannot be more than twenty-eight degrees away from the Sun, so it will be in the preceding sign, the same sign as the Sun, or the following sign. Mercury is closely related to the Sun, so we align our interpretation of Mercury with that of the Sun sign, as shown on these pages.

♈ MERCURY IN ARIES

THIS PLACING makes people positive and optimistic, decisive and quick-thinking, and ready for assertive action. If Mercury is in negative aspect to Mars, subjects can be over-impulsive and hasty. They love debate and argument but fine detail will bore them, and sustaining concentration can be a problem.

Sun-sign Pisces, Mercury in Aries These people have a very lively imagination, and creative potential will be easily expressed. Emotions run high, and if Mercury has a negative aspect to the Moon or Uranus, the subject's moods may swing between optimism and uncertainty. Typically weak Piscean willpower will be strengthened.

Sun-sign Aries, Mercury in Aries Although they will have very little patience, positive, clear thinking will be quickly applied in any situation. An Arien trait is the need for immediate action, but they must learn to avoid impulsive responses.

Sun-sign Taurus, Mercury in Aries A beneficial placing that will bestow a spirit of enterprise. It spices up the usual stability of Taurus and there will be much less caution and more assertion. The Taurean talent for careful planning will still be evident, but there will be less patience. Criticism, however constructive, may provoke irritation.

The Influence of Mercury
Mercury was the messenger of the gods, and the planet rules the intellect and communication.

♉ MERCURY IN TAURUS

INFLEXIBILITY WILL BE a characteristic of those with Mercury in Taurus, particularly an inability to change the mind. Common sense will be present, as will the ability to plan constructively. The mind may be slightly slow, but steady and careful.

Sun-sign Aries, Mercury in Taurus Impetuous Ariens profit from this placing of Mercury, which acts as a stabilizer, enabling them to think constructively before acting. Common sense is strong, and there are great powers of concentration.

Sun-sign Taurus, Mercury in Taurus Straightforward, if stubborn, these characters are dependable. They dislike change, and need time to get used to new ideas. Sometimes they can appear slow-minded because they like to take their time; nothing will be hurried.

Sun-sign Gemini, Mercury in Taurus Mercury rules Gemini, and its effect is strong and in this case beneficial, steadying the subject and enabling him or her to act with deliberation. These people assimilate facts easily, and have practical common sense along with the natural Geminian liveliness and versatility.

♊ MERCURY IN GEMINI

FROM ONE OF the two signs it rules, Mercury's influence will be strong. Communication will be necessary for these people and they like to be heard as well as seen. They make decisions quickly, but changing their mind is common. Superficiality can be a fault; craftiness a possibility.

Sun-sign Taurus, Mercury in Gemini Taureans will be less sluggish when Mercury is in Gemini. They will be more versatile than other Taureans, but lack none of the typical Taurean determination and sense of purpose.

Sun-sign Gemini, Mercury in Gemini Those Gemini characteristics related to Mercury – quickness of thought and versatility, as well as intense curiosity – will be strengthened by this placing, as will faults such as superficiality and restlessness.

Sun-sign Cancer, Mercury in Gemini
Mercurial changes of mind should match Cancerian changes of mood, but an element of Gemini scepticism will challenge emotional responses, and the imagination will be less likely to get out of hand.

♋ MERCURY IN CANCER

PEOPLE WHO HAVE Mercury in Cancer tend to look back rather than forward – an inbuilt sense of nostalgia combines with a mistrust of the future. When their emotional response clashes with their logical thinking they find it very difficult to assess situations. The Sun and Moon signs should indicate whether these individuals will be tenacious or hesitant in their approach to life.

Sun-sign Gemini, Mercury in Cancer
These Geminians are very intuitive and tend to act instinctively. They are likely to be more sympathetic than critical, and more sensitive than intolerant. Their tendency to be changeable will need to be fought.

Sun-sign Cancer, Mercury in Cancer
Instinct and intuition are strong and can be trusted. The imagination is vivid and should be used creatively. Moodiness may be a problem, and pessimism and depression may be emphasized if they are suggested in other areas of the horoscope.

Sun-sign Leo, Mercury in Cancer
Leos with this placing will be less dogmatic than usual; Mercury will make them kind and considerate, as well as cautious and shrewd. Strong emotions will ensure that they are admirable lovers, while Leonine optimism will curb the Cancerian tendency to worry.

♌ MERCURY IN LEO

PEOPLE WITH THIS placing tend to be dogmatic, but their organizational ability will be admirable. Excellent powers of concentration are usually apparent, but they can sometimes be unwittingly condescending.

Sun-sign Cancer, Mercury in Leo
These Cancerians are excellent organizers. Positive and rational, they will be tenacious in sticking to any path they have decided to follow. They will sometimes be surprisingly forceful.

Sun-sign Leo, Mercury in Leo
While there will be excellent powers of leadership and the useful ability to get things done, the presence of dogmatism and an imperious attitude to others will be increased by this placing of Mercury, and verbally, they tend to exaggerate.

Sun-sign Virgo, Mercury in Leo
Mercury rules Virgo, and will work powerfully for these individuals, helping to temper any lack of self-confidence, and giving a stronger, more optimistic outlook on life.

♍ MERCURY IN VIRGO

THIS IS ONE OF the two signs ruled by Mercury, from which its influence is very firm indeed. Great analytical ability is conferred on an individual by this placing, as well as innate practicality and common sense. There is a tendency to follow the path expected of oneself rather than to think out an individual course. There may also be too much concern with detail, which can obscure the overall view of a situation.

Sun-sign Leo, Mercury in Virgo
The over-enthusiastic side of Leo will be governed rather than negated by this placing, which adds common sense and encourages these people to think twice before boasting or exaggerating. The nervous energy of Mercury combines well with Leonine emotional and physical energy, and creative flair can be used to gain financial success.

Sun-sign Virgo, Mercury in Virgo
This will be a strongly Virgoan person with an excellent mind, capable of detailed, analytical work, but who must guard against worry and the tendency to be over-finicky. Self-criticism will sap confidence and encourage shyness, while nervous haste can occasionally lead to carelessness. Relaxation techniques may be useful to help curb tension.

Sun-sign Libra, Mercury in Virgo
Versatility, common sense, and a critical turn of mind will combat the Libran tendency towards indecision and procrastination. Libran laziness should not be a problem, and there will be a desire for a lively social life. This is a good combination provided that Venus is not also in Virgo.

The Orrery
This painting by Joseph Wright (1734–1797) depicts an orrery – a clockwork model of the solar system popular in the 18th century.

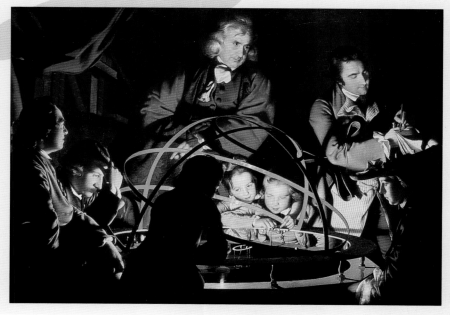

PLANETS

☉ SUN

☽ MOON

☿ MERCURY

♀ VENUS

♂ MARS

♃ JUPITER

♄ SATURN

♅ URANUS

♆ NEPTUNE

♇ PLUTO

SIGNS

♈ ARIES

♉ TAURUS

♊ GEMINI

♋ CANCER

♌ LEO

♍ VIRGO

♎ LIBRA

♏ SCORPIO

♐ SAGITTARIUS

♑ CAPRICORN

♒ AQUARIUS

♓ PISCES

PLANETS

SUN

MOON

MERCURY

VENUS

MARS

JUPITER

SATURN

URANUS

NEPTUNE

PLUTO

SIGNS

ARIES

TAURUS

GEMINI

CANCER

LEO

VIRGO

LIBRA

SCORPIO

SAGITTARIUS

CAPRICORN

AQUARIUS

PISCES

MERCURY IN LIBRA

PROCRASTINATION AND indecision are likely to have their effect under this influence of Mercury. These people prefer to achieve without effort. The powers of concentration will not be strong (though positive aspects between the Sun, Moon, and Saturn will help). People with this placing will go to any lengths to avoid controversy, and will be helped in this aim by their natural charm.

Sun-sign Virgo, Mercury in Libra Little of the rather typical Virgoan tendency to worry should show itself, for the attitude to life will be serene and cool. There is an enviable ability to relax. The subject may tend to be over-critical, but an appeal to fairness should succeed. Indecision should be countered.
Sun-sign Libra, Mercury in Libra Indecision will be a way of life for these people, as may mental laziness. Nagging will not help; gentle encouragement to recognize their own achievements is needed. Procrastination will be a problem.
Sun-sign Scorpio, Mercury in Libra These Sun-sign Scorpios have a greater ability than usual to listen sympathetically to others. Their minds work well, but less incisively than those of other Scorpios.

They brood less over personal problems, and find it easy to talk about them with partners or friends.

MERCURY IN SCORPIO

THIS IS USUALLY an excellent placing, for Mercurial logic and rationality combine well with Scorpio intensity and intuition. Mercury is not very communicative from this sign, and the subject will be more inward-looking than usual, tending to conceal problems. Determination and a passion for getting to the core of problems will be a strong feature.

Sun-sign Libra, Mercury in Scorpio Determination, sense of purpose, and intuition will mark out these subjects – though they may seem indecisive because of a reluctance to take action. Objectives are achieved once action is taken. There may be a tendency to plot and scheme.
Sun-sign Scorpio, Mercury in Scorpio Intellectual powers will be second to none, and be married to formidable determination and sense of purpose. A compelling interest of some kind is essential if these strengths are not to be wasted in jealousy or resentfulness.
Sun-sign Sagittarius, Mercury in Scorpio Sagittarians usually dislike working in detail; this placing will moderate that failing, reducing impetuosity and regulating natural enthusiasm with a little caution. Mercury will slightly dampen (but by no means extinguish) Sagittarian fire, and is likely to sharpen the sense of humour. Scorpio adds depth to someone who is basically concerned with the overall breadth of problems and situations.

Gemini's Ruling Planet
This 17th-century Persian painting depicts the Twins, the symbol of Gemini, which is ruled by Mercury.

MERCURY IN SAGITTARIUS

TRADITIONALLY, Mercury is said to work poorly from Sagittarius, but if superficiality, restlessness, and a tendency to be over-optimistic can be kept in check, there are benefits. The constant search for intellectual stimulation, for instance, can often be highly fruitful, although the temptation to flit from one subject to another, so that none are properly studied, should be avoided. There is also considerable breadth of vision, and probably a flair for languages.

Sun-sign Scorpio, Mercury in Sagittarius Mercury will lighten and stimulate the intensity of Scorpio, making the character less grave and ponderous, and not so likely to be absorbed by personal problems. Broadmindedness and an optimistic outlook will be refreshing, and these emotional, intuitive subjects will be more positive and reasonable than other Scorpios. Interests and hobbies will be imaginatively pursued.
Sun-sign Sagittarius, Mercury in Sagittarius This is an extremely spirited combination – too lively, some astrologers would say. It must certainly be balanced and controlled if it is not to carry the subject away on a tide of Sagittarian enthusiasm. Look for Saturn in the chart to see if there is help there. Optimism can turn to a total belief in "pie in the sky"; enthusiasm will quickly fizzle out if plans are not rapidly realized. Restlessness – especially mental restlessness – needs to be combated, and physical exercise is a necessity.
Sun-sign Capricorn, Mercury in Sagittarius A favourable placing for Capricorns, who will be less single-mindedly intent on career and personal development than other Capricorns. They will also be relatively relaxed and easy-going – and much better able to cope with setbacks without grumbling. Over-optimism will be tempered, but there will still be great enthusiasm for life. The sense of humour will be particularly engaging.

♑ MERCURY IN CAPRICORN

THESE CHARACTERS are strong and silent, determined and decisive. Their word is their bond, and they have a matter-of-fact approach. They are constructive and practical, forming a rational, cool view of every situation. Every move will be carefully calculated and made with thought and caution. They may be pessimistic, but are ambitious, and personal goals are usually achieved.

Sun-sign Sagittarius, Mercury in Capricorn In this case, Sagittarian over-enthusiasm is balanced by common sense and a cautious streak. Capricorn irony combines to devastating effect with Sagittarian broad humour, and can be used to advantage. Restlessness may be less of a problem than with some Sun-sign Sagittarians, but the degree of versatility may be less notable.

Sun-sign Capricorn, Mercury in Capricorn Vigorous ambition and a positive outlook make it easy for these Capricorns to deal with rivals. The mind works in a very calculated and careful way and there is often mathematical and scientific ability, and occasionally musical talent.

Sun-sign Aquarius, Mercury in Capricorn Aquarian perversity is curbed by Capricorn practicality, and stubbornness is also less of a problem. Unconventionality will be tempered, and there may be a flair for science. The intellect will be fired by the imagination.

♒ MERCURY IN AQUARIUS

ORIGINALITY CAN be accompanied by inflexibility and perversity. Nervous tension may cause problems, and relaxation may prove difficult. The subject can be stubborn and perverse when under stress. The mind is extremely quick, and there will be an intellectual approach to problems, which will be precisely assessed. Aquarian humanitarianism will be highlighted in this sign.

Sun-sign Capricorn, Mercury in Aquarius These people are highly individualistic in both lifestyle and personality, but will also feel the strong Capricornian desire for tradition in all its forms. Subjects need to know themselves before this conflict can be resolved. This placing of Mercury also adds a lively streak to what can often be a rather serious disposition.

Sun-sign Aquarius, Mercury in Aquarius Great originality, a daunting stubbornness, and considerable perversity and unpredictability are all likely – but also objectivity, friendliness, and the desire to be helpful. Flexibility of judgement should be developed.

Sun-sign Pisces, Mercury in Aquarius These people are great humanitarians, but are less likely than many Sun-sign Pisceans to be overwhelmed by their feelings. Their natural intuition is controlled by Mercurial logic, and they can use their imagination creatively.

♓ MERCURY IN PISCES

PEOPLE WITH this placing of Mercury can be highly intuitive, but extremely disorganized, forgetful, and careless. They are exceptionally kind and sympathetic by nature, and will do anything for anyone. Happily, their strong intuition is usually correct, for their lack of organizational ability can lead to confusion that they often find very difficult to resolve. They have a highly vivid imagination that too often works negatively, for they can invent extraordinary falsehoods attempting to get themselves out of trouble.

The Heavens and the Zodiac
In this 15th-century illustration from Barthélemy l'Anglais' Livre sur la proprieté des choses, *the signs of the zodiac revolve around the Earth.*

Sun-sign Aquarius, Mercury in Pisces The emotional level of a Sun-sign Aquarian is heightened when Mercury is at work from Pisces, and Aquarian unpredictability is less evident. Mercury makes these people more sensitive to the feelings of others. An original imagination will need a positive outlet.

Sun-sign Pisces, Mercury in Pisces Confusion and muddle tend to surround these people, although (or maybe because) they have wonderful imaginations that can lift them out of the rut of everyday life and into the stratosphere of fancy. This imagination should be channelled and constructively employed.

Sun-sign Aries, Mercury in Pisces Arien selfishness and assertiveness is softened by this position of Mercury, but decisiveness will be less sure, and these people tend to be forgetful. The emotional level of Aries will be increased, and is less likely to be expressed in unexpected flashes of anger.

Mercury glyph

PLANETS
☉ SUN
☽ MOON
☿ MERCURY
♀ VENUS
♂ MARS
♃ JUPITER
♄ SATURN
♅ URANUS
♆ NEPTUNE
♇ PLUTO

SIGNS
♈ ARIES
♉ TAURUS
♊ GEMINI
♋ CANCER
♌ LEO
♍ VIRGO
♎ LIBRA
♏ SCORPIO
♐ SAGITTARIUS
♑ CAPRICORN
♒ AQUARIUS
♓ PISCES

PLANETS
SUN
MOON
MERCURY
VENUS
MARS
JUPITER
SATURN
URANUS
NEPTUNE
PLUTO

SIGNS
ARIES
TAURUS
GEMINI
CANCER
LEO
VIRGO
LIBRA
SCORPIO
SAGITTARIUS
CAPRICORN
AQUARIUS
PISCES

VENUS THROUGH THE SIGNS

Venus is known, astronomically, as the second inferior planet, and can never be more than forty-eight degrees from the Sun as seen from the Earth. It will therefore share the same sign as the Sun or be in one of the two signs either side of it; for example, in a chart with a Gemini Sun sign, Venus will be in either Aries or Taurus, in Gemini with the Sun, or in Cancer or Leo. Venus influences the way we relate to other people and our attitudes to money and possessions. When reading this section, first look up the relevant sign placing of Venus, then read the paragraph relating it to the Sun sign in question.

♈ VENUS IN ARIES

VENUS IN ARIES indicates someone who can be rather aggressive in his or her emotional expression. Usually the pursuer rather than the pursued, these people are enthusiastic but selfish lovers. Their attitude towards money is enterprising and risks may be taken.

Sun-sign Aquarius, Venus in Aries Emotional attachments will be strong, but there will be hesitation when it comes to committing to a permanent relationship. There will be a taste for unusual possessions.
Sun-sign Pisces, Venus in Aries Ardent lovers, these Pisceans will continually strive for a rewarding relationship, which they need for psychological completeness. They enjoy money too much to save it.
Sun-sign Aries, Venus in Aries Passionate, but very determined to maintain independence, these people can also be selfish at times. Impulse buying will sap their finances.
Sun-sign Taurus, Venus in Aries The passion of these sensual lovers means that romance will have memorable heights of excitement. Possessiveness is a problem, and a love of luxury can prove expensive.
Sun-sign Gemini, Venus in Aries The Gemini mistrust of emotion may fight against Arien passion, but if this problem can be solved the sexual life will be satisfying, with friendship an important element.

The Influence of Venus
Venus, named after the Roman goddess of love, rules Taurus and Libra. Venus' influence extends to art and money.

♉ VENUS IN TAURUS

VENUS RULES TAURUS and is strong in this sign, making subjects romantic and affectionate if somewhat passive lovers. Taurean possessiveness can be a problem. They prefer to make money without too much effort.

Sun-sign Pisces, Venus in Taurus This placing produces a practical approach to love. Stability makes the subjects excellent, if possessive, friends and lovers. Creative flair can be turned to good financial effect.
Sun-sign Aries, Venus in Taurus These people tend to be extremely passionate, but they approach love affairs cautiously, and selfishness is an unfortunate trait. Enthusiasm and prudence are combined, in both love and finance.
Sun-sign Taurus, Venus in Taurus Taurean traits will be much stronger than usual, and there will be a need to acquire material possessions in order to feel emotionally secure.
Sun-sign Gemini, Venus in Taurus These people can be emotional and affectionate unless the Gemini influence takes over, when emotion can be over-intellectualized. Geminian wit combined with Taurean shrewdness should result in enhanced income.
Sun-sign Cancer, Venus in Taurus The Cancerian tendency to cherish, meeting Taurean possessiveness can be cloying for partners. Cancerian shrewdness and Venusian flair leads to superb business potential.

♊ VENUS IN GEMINI

THESE FLIRTATIOUS people need partners who are intellectually as well as sexually stimulating. They are reluctant to settle down but are capable of sustained devotion. They have a flair for money-making.

Sun-sign Aries, Venus in Gemini The ardent passion and selfishness of Aries meeting the light-hearted Geminian attitude to love implies an above-average chance of infidelity.
Sun-sign Taurus, Venus in Gemini Taurus' usual capacity for love is enhanced, the personality lightened and given vitality by this placing.

These people will be quick-thinking and formidable in business.

Sun-sign Gemini, Venus in Gemini
Love affairs can be inhibited by the tendency to over-analyze emotions. Quick wits help financial success.

Sun-sign Cancer, Venus in Gemini
This placing adds a rational streak that enables Cancerians to be very objective when choosing partners. They are shrewd in business, too.

Sun-sign Leo, Venus in Gemini
Emotionally generous, the need for love is spiced with flirtatiousness in these Leos. Extravagance is usually matched by fiscal astuteness.

VENUS IN CANCER

VENUS IN CANCER makes people fearful of change and although they enjoy emotional involvement it can create a claustrophobic atmosphere. Subjects are careful with money.

Sun-sign Taurus, Venus in Cancer
Sensuality is passionately conveyed, but there can be storms caused by possessiveness. Subjects must learn to let go when an affair finishes.

Sun-sign Gemini, Venus in Cancer
Cool Geminian emotions will be heightened by this combination. Financial security can be attained by a talent for collecting artefacts.

Sun-sign Cancer, Venus in Cancer
A tendency to worry over a partner can be a problem as all the elements of Venus in Cancer are emphasized. There is shrewdness in business.

Sun-sign Leo, Venus in Cancer
This placing encourages a rewarding sex life, but makes Leos emotionally sensitive. Security is important.

Sun-sign Virgo, Venus in Cancer
These reserved Virgoans have strong emotional resources but may find it difficult to express them. They are clever, but miserly with money.

VENUS IN LEO

LOYAL AND FAITHFUL, fiery and passionate, these people will enjoy an exuberant sex life but should

be careful not to dominate their partners. They love luxury and quality, and are shrewd investors.

Sun-sign Gemini, Venus in Leo
Fun-loving if unfaithful partners, sexual as well as social variety is needed. Extravagance and impulse-buying may be problems.

Sun-sign Cancer, Venus in Leo
Exuberance meets moodiness, while short temper may combine with bossiness. Constancy and loyalty in a partner will be important.

Sun-sign Leo, Venus in Leo
These Leos will support their partners, but should avoid over-extravagant behaviour. Money will be spent to ensure comfort at home.

Sun-sign Virgo, Venus in Leo
Virgoan modesty clashes with Leo assurance and subjects become over-talkative when nervous. Financial recklessness will be enjoyed.

Sun-sign Libra, Venus in Leo
These romantic Librans are very sensual, but may try to buy a lover's affection with extravagant presents.

VENUS IN VIRGO

SEXUAL INHIBITION WILL need to be overcome if a partnership is to work; when it is conquered, Venus in Virgo produces an enormously attractive person with natural grace and modesty. See the positions of the Sun, Moon, Ascendant, and Mars to illuminate the situation.

Sun-sign Cancer, Venus in Virgo
Virgo's critical nature combined with Cancerian moodiness means these people need to learn to relax. They are unwilling to spend money.

Sun-sign Leo, Venus in Virgo
Leonine exuberance will be toned down and self-assurance may be lacking. Leo bossiness combined with Virgoan criticism can alienate others.

Sun-sign Virgo, Venus in Virgo
Efforts must be made to overcome the sexual inhibitions caused by Virgoan modesty. Money will only be spent with great caution.

Sun-sign Libra, Venus in Virgo
The Virgoan difficulty in expressing love may conflict with the Libran need for a fulfilling partnership. Finance is practically handled.

Sun-sign Scorpio, Venus in Virgo
Sex may be considered a forbidden subject, making relationships difficult – aspects to the Moon, Ascendant, and Mars, may help. Friendship will be highly valued.

The Constellations
This star map of Taurus, which is ruled by Venus, is from an 18th-century constellation book.

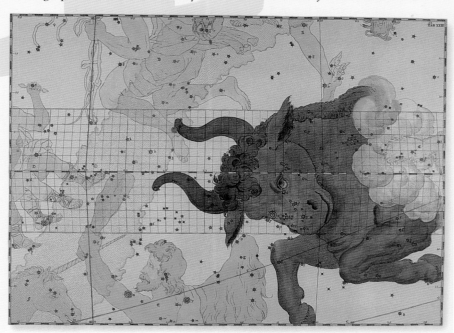

PLANETS
SUN
MOON
MERCURY
VENUS
MARS
JUPITER
SATURN
URANUS
NEPTUNE
PLUTO
SIGNS
ARIES
TAURUS
GEMINI
CANCER
LEO
VIRGO
LIBRA
SCORPIO
SAGITTARIUS
CAPRICORN
AQUARIUS
PISCES

PLANETS

SUN

MOON

MERCURY

VENUS

MARS

JUPITER

SATURN

URANUS

NEPTUNE

PLUTO

SIGNS

ARIES

TAURUS

GEMINI

CANCER

LEO

VIRGO

LIBRA

SCORPIO

SAGITTARIUS

CAPRICORN

AQUARIUS

PISCES

VENUS IN LIBRA

VENUS IS STRONG from this sign, encouraging a romantic, idealistic view of love. There is a need for a partnership, and the subject may not feel "whole" until one is established. There may be a temptation to spend money in order to buy love.

Sun-sign Leo, Venus in Libra
There will be a tendency to put lovers on a pedestal, with disillusion ensuing when they fall off. These Leos will be rather laid-back, and will readily spend money to make life comfortable and enjoyable.

Sun-sign Virgo, Venus in Libra
Venus in this position helps Virgoans to relax and enjoy every aspect of being in love. It will also make them less critical and more sympathetic. They are prepared to work hard, and enjoy spending on pleasure.

Sun-sign Libra, Venus in Libra
Venus' influence will be strong and all of the Libran romantic and affectionate attributes will be emphasized. This will be especially noticeable if the Sun and Venus are in conjunction. Laziness and extravagance may be a problem.

Sun-sign Scorpio, Venus in Libra
The intense passion of Scorpio will be coloured by romance, and there will be a more obvious sympathy with and understanding of partners. Jealousy may be a complication.

Sun-sign Sagittarius, Venus in Libra
Sagittarians always enjoy the chase, but in this case will have a sense of romance that gives them a more loving attitude to their prey. There will be less emotional restlessness, and creature comforts and financial security will be important.

VENUS IN SCORPIO

VENUS IS AT its sexiest in this sign, and sexuality and a love of romance will need to be expressed. Though Scorpio jealousy may show itself, the happiness of a harmonious relationship will be enhanced by the positive expression of sexuality. Other interests will be needed to satisfy the energy of this placing, which also shows financial ability.

Sun-sign Virgo, Venus in Scorpio
If these Virgoans can relax and enjoy their sensuality, this placing of Venus will be helpful; inhibited Virgoans may be confused by it and try to suppress their attractiveness. Money is managed well.

Sun-sign Libra, Venus in Scorpio
Venus will add intensity and sense of purpose to Librans in love. Sexuality will be increased, somewhat tempering the romantic attitude of Libra. They will make money, and enjoy spending it.

Sun-sign Scorpio, Venus in Scorpio
Romantic overtones will add to the sexual glamour of these irresistible Scorpios. Everything about Venus in Scorpio will be emphasized, but they may be jealous to the point of obsession.

Sun-sign Sagittarius, Venus in Scorpio Lively, fiery sexuality will be enhanced, but these Sagittarians can be plagued by jealousy. They are susceptible to financial risk-taking.

Venus at her Toilette
Venus is associated with beauty and sensuality as well as love.

VENUS IN SAGITTARIUS

A GREAT NEED for independence will be felt by people with Venus in Sagittarius, and it may cause them to hesitate before they personally commit themselves. The sign is a dual one, and more than one relationship at a time is quite likely. Money will be easy come, easy go.

Sun-sign Libra, Venus in Sagittarius
The need for intellectual as well as sexual satisfaction is high, and these Librans will be very romantic. Friendship and intellectual rapport will be emphasized. Professional help with finance is advisable.

Sun-sign Scorpio, Venus in Sagittarius The intensity of Scorpio sexuality will be lightened by this position of Venus. Scorpio jealousy may conflict with Sagittarian need for independence. Any gambling instincts must be controlled.

Sun-sign Sagittarius, Venus in Sagittarius All the attributes of Venus in Sagittarius tend to be emphasized, and the chase will be enjoyed as much as the capture. If Neptune is also in Sagittarius there will be a strong romantic streak. Money will slip through the fingers.

Sun-sign Capricorn, Venus in Sagittarius Over-cool Capricorn emotion will be warmed by Venus, but a partner must be prepared to support Capricorn ambition and contribute intellectual stimulation. Money-making is less important than usual for these Capricorns.

Sun-sign Aquarius, Venus in Sagittarius The fire of Sagittarius will warm the somewhat distant charm of Aquarians, but they will still not be eager to rush into a permanent relationship. Money will be spent on fashionable items.

Sun-sign Capricorn, Venus in Scorpio Love will be taken very seriously, but deep feelings may be difficult to express. Commitment may be slow to come, but will be loyally upheld. Steady financial growth should be achieved.

♑ VENUS IN CAPRICORN

HERE ARE EXTREMELY faithful lovers, who must ensure that their cool sensuality does not prevent their partners from realizing they are loved. Sometimes a partner will be chosen as a status symbol or for material gain, but in a loving relationship Capricorn ambition needs to be shared with the partner, with the alliance geared to personal and financial development.

Sun-sign Scorpio, Venus in Capricorn These Scorpios almost always get what they desire, but they rarely consider what their partner wants. Ruthlessness can be a strong characteristic of the personality. Business acumen is likely to be considerable, but remorseless.

Sun-sign Sagittarius, Venus in Capricorn Likely to be more faithful than most Sagittarians, these people can be plagued by conflicting desires. They need a great deal of freedom but also prefer to be in a conventional relationship. Clever and calculated risk-taking can result in an excellent income.

Sun-sign Capricorn, Venus in Capricorn Ambition for material progress is powerful, and can exclude concern for the partner and family. Characteristics of Venus in Capricorn will be emphasized, and great faithfulness and loyalty will be part of a reserved personality.

Sun-sign Aquarius, Venus in Capricorn Despite magnetic powers of attraction, these individuals are not romantic, nor do they like to commit themselves to a permanent relationship. A sense of balance is needed in financial affairs since poor management of money is usual.

Sun-sign Pisces, Venus in Capricorn If the coolness of Venus in this position is not allowed to inhibit the individual, this can be an excellent placing, having a steadying influence on what can sometimes be rather overwhelming Piscean affection. Financial advice may be necessary if Mercury is also in Pisces.

♒ VENUS IN AQUARIUS

PEOPLE WITH Venus in Aquarius usually possess a cool, romantic glamour that others find highly attractive. They enjoy romance, but often they are not prepared for a relationship with all the compromises and obligations that ensue. These people make kind and thoughtful friends, and are likely to be financially astute.

Sun-sign Sagittarius, Venus in Aquarius The ardent passion of Sagittarius is cooled by Venus, although individuals will, once they are committed, be faithful. Rash decisions are likely to be made regarding money.

Sun-sign Capricorn, Venus in Aquarius Capricorns with this placing find it difficult to express their emotions, and can appear haughty. Relationships may suffer because they feel no partner is quite good enough for them. Caution interferes with spending money on pleasure.

Sun-sign Aquarius, Venus in Aquarius Magnetically attractive, but almost impossible to know well, in these individuals all the traits of Venus in Aquarius are exaggerated. They like to buy expensive luxuries.

Sun-sign Pisces, Venus in Aquarius Intuition helps these Pisceans to choose a lover, and emotion is balanced by Aquarian caution. Financial advice may be needed.

Sun-sign Aries, Venus in Aquarius Cool Venus will dampen the fiery passion of Aries, and the desire for commitment may conflict with a need for freedom. Financial flair is likely to be marred by hasty investments.

♓ VENUS IN PISCES

EMOTION WILL FIGURE in every decision made by someone with Venus in Pisces. These people can be easy prey to the unscrupulous, in love and elsewhere. If problems arise they prefer to opt for the easiest solution.

Sun-sign Capricorn, Venus in Pisces Warmer and much more affectionate to partners than many Capricorns, these subjects enjoy spending time with their family, and worry less about material affairs. Intuition concerning finance is reliable.

Sun-sign Aquarius, Venus in Pisces The humanitarian qualities of Aquarius will be underlined, and the emotions warmed – these people are less distant than other Aquarians. Money is handled unwisely.

Sun-sign Pisces, Venus in Pisces Pisceans with Venus in the same sign make well-meaning sacrifices that are often too great. They are excessively generous, which can land them in financial trouble.

Sun-sign Aries, Venus in Pisces The fire of Aries adds strength and assertiveness to the tenderness of Pisces. These Ariens are unselfish and sympathetic, but they can be financially over-enterprising.

Sun-sign Taurus, Venus in Pisces Emotional security is important to these Taureans, who express themselves passionately. They tend to spend too much on their creature comforts.

Venus de Milo
This Greek sculpture of the goddess Venus dates from the end of the second century BC.

Venus glyph

PLANETS
SUN
MOON
MERCURY
VENUS
MARS
JUPITER
SATURN
URANUS
NEPTUNE
PLUTO
SIGNS
ARIES
TAURUS
GEMINI
CANCER
LEO
VIRGO
LIBRA
SCORPIO
SAGITTARIUS
CAPRICORN
AQUARIUS
PISCES

PLANETS

SUN

MOON

MERCURY

VENUS

MARS

JUPITER

SATURN

URANUS

NEPTUNE

PLUTO

SIGNS

ARIES

TAURUS

GEMINI

CANCER

LEO

VIRGO

LIBRA

SCORPIO

SAGITTARIUS

CAPRICORN

AQUARIUS

PISCES

MARS through the Signs

The orbit of Mars is further from the Sun than that of the Earth, therefore it can fall in any sign of the zodiac (unlike Mercury and Venus, which are always relatively near the Sun). Mars influences our energy levels, assertiveness, competitiveness, and sex drive. It also shows how easily we are roused to anger, for it governs the flow of adrenalin in our systems. Mars' energies can be used both positively and negatively. To determine which way a subject is likely to use them, you must consider the sign in which it falls, as well as the aspects that Mars receives from other planets.

MARS IN ARIES

MARS RULES ARIES, and when it is in that sign in a birth chart, it works very powerfully, and is a focal point of the horoscope. It heightens the level of physical energy, and if this is not expressed through some kind of exercise, such as sport, the individual will feel restless and unfulfilled.

People with this influence in their chart will be confident and assertive, wanting (and needing) to win. They take a strong line if there is a hint of hesitation in anyone they live or work with, forcing the other person into action without taking account of his or her feelings. They have a powerful sex drive, which they express in an uninhibited fashion.

In general, this is an invigorating influence, and individuals with this element in their horoscope should have a number of interests into which their energy can be poured. Outbursts of Martian temper should be avoided if possible. If Mars aspects Saturn, Uranus, or Pluto, the flow of energy may be inhibited.

MARS IN TAURUS

THESE PEOPLE WORK tenaciously in their career and leisure activities. An abundant sex drive will be warmly expressed – although there may be a strong element of possessiveness. The energy level will be high, and

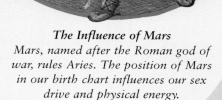

The Influence of Mars
Mars, named after the Roman god of war, rules Aries. The position of Mars in our birth chart influences our sex drive and physical energy.

(provided that Mars is not afflicted) used in a controlled way. Taurean patience will steady the Martian quick temper, but once aroused, the storm will be robust, and the rebuke will often be expressed much too vigorously, damaging an emotional or professional relationship.

One problem with all this energy is that it can turn into stubbornness, and Mars will certainly strengthen this trait if it is indicated elsewhere in the birth chart. In a chart that is dominated by earth signs, the more adventurous facets of Mars will be somewhat repressed, or at any event slowed down. The Taurean need for financial security will be evident, and a great deal of energy will be spent in making money. This is a splendid placing for those who enjoy robust sports, and good too for dancers and athletes since it bestows discipline and strength. The throat is likely to be vulnerable to infections.

MARS IN GEMINI

IT IS IMPORTANT for people with this placing of Mars to exercise the body as well as the mind – but they may not be eager to do this unless some sort of intellectual challenge is involved, and may find exercise boring. Some astrologers suggest that Mars is not "well placed" in Gemini because it tends not to be very invigorating physically. However, it will certainly stimulate and enliven the mind.

Gemini-Mars individuals should be encouraged to find an exercise that satisfies physical and mental needs. If not, restlessness may well result, which is often expressed as short temper and irritability – directed towards the self as well as outwardly. Energy is expended somewhat randomly, both on a day-to-day basis and in the general pattern of the whole life. Frequent changes of occupation will actually be beneficial, and versatility and flexibility should be given full rein.

These people are sexually lively, treat the subject light-heartedly, and have an interest in experimentation. They will be very energetic lovers, and should enjoy a rewarding sexual life that will last into their old age.

♋ MARS IN CANCER

THIS POSITION OF Mars powerfully influences the love life and sex life, and lovers with Mars in Cancer will be sensual and caring, instinctively knowing how to please a partner. However, there is the possibility that they will work too hard at the relationship and create a cloying atmosphere. Any project they decide to undertake that needs physical or emotional energy will be seen through to completion, though there may be physical stress and tension if Mars receives negative aspects from the Sun, Moon, or Uranus.

These people can have short tempers, and in moments of anger may express themselves harshly, even cruelly. Cancer enhances the memory, therefore it will not be easy for them to forgive and forget any offence, and there may be lingering resentment which they find difficult to erase from their mind. Irrational fretting will only exacerbate their problems, and they should try to talk them through with other people. The acquisition of a home and family will be very important, and they will make every effort to support them.

The best type of exercise for those with Mars in Cancer is some form of water sport – water is a symbol of the emotions and for Cancer an excellent relaxing agent.

♌ MARS IN LEO

THE FIERY ENTHUSIASM, energy, and assertiveness of Mars is well suited to Leo, and people with this placing of the planet will have an immense love of life, and will also be eager for others to enjoy themselves. Powers of leadership will be strong, but individuals must guard against being overly assertive and pushy, especially when dealing with those less assured than themselves.

There will be a keen sense of drama, which again needs to be carefully controlled if it is not to expand and become showiness, exaggeration, and bombast. These people do not suffer pompousness or self-indulgence gladly, and small-mindedness and pettiness will be deeply despised, sometimes to the point of rudeness. The quick temper of Mars is flaring and passionate, but at least Leonine magnanimity ensures that any clash is quickly forgiven and forgotten.

The sex life will be enthusiastic, colourful, and rewarding, and there may well be a creative passion for art. If Mars is negatively aspected by Saturn, energy may be unevenly spent, but provided that more sober elements of the horoscope help the subject to use the energy in a controlled way, this placing is wonderfully invigorating physically, and these people are likely to enjoy robust health. There may be minor trouble with the spine, especially if days are spent at an office desk, and yoga or the Alexander technique might help. Leo rules the heart, so aerobic exercise such as swimming or dancing is recommended.

♍ MARS IN VIRGO

THE VIRGO INFLUENCE on Martian energy is to constrict and tighten it, and with this placing of Mars a generous measure of nervous energy can make an individual edgy, tense, and restless. This will be counteracted if there are positive aspects to Mars from the Sun, Moon, Mercury, or Venus.

Virgo-Mars individuals will be hard and willing workers, particularly good at tasks that require painstaking study, but occasionally there will be too much attention to detail and too little to the grand design. Lack of self-confidence can sap ambition, and it is not always easy for these individuals to carry responsibility – at least for a long period of time. Their need for constant activity should be satisfied by a well-organized, steady routine, covering both work and leisure hours. Time for real relaxation must be included, for this too is highly important. Yoga or stretching exercises are likely to help.

The combination of Mars and Virgo is not helpful to the sex life: Virgo is a discriminating sign, and the kind of refinement it encourages is not likely to marry well with the positive demands of Mars. Look at the position of Venus in the horoscope, and to the Venus sign itself, to see if they offer help (this will certainly be the case if, for instance, Venus is well placed, or makes a positive aspect to Mars).

If Mars receives negative aspects from the Sun, Mercury, or Uranus, the subject will find it very difficult to unwind, and the result can be growing tension, leading to nervous stomach upsets or migraine. Skin allergies can be exacerbated by tension. Cycling or jogging, or other forms of strenuous exercise, will help to disperse excess energy.

Nicolaus Copernicus
Copernicus made a breakthrough in the 16th century when he suggested that the Sun is the centre of our solar system.

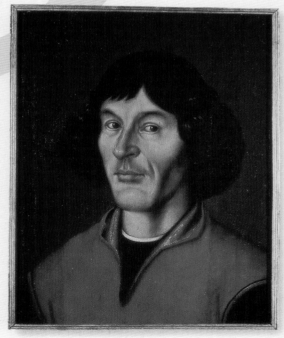

PLANETS

SUN

MOON

MERCURY

VENUS

MARS

JUPITER

SATURN

URANUS

NEPTUNE

PLUTO

SIGNS

ARIES

TAURUS

GEMINI

CANCER

LEO

VIRGO

LIBRA

SCORPIO

SAGITTARIUS

CAPRICORN

AQUARIUS

PISCES

♎ MARS IN LIBRA

ALTHOUGH MARS boosts the sexual energy when it is in Libra, the individual will still have a somewhat ambiguous attitude to love-making – one day enthusiastic and energetic, the next lethargic and lackadaisical. Plenty of excuses will be on hand for inaction, but the simple truth is that these people blow hot and cold, passionate and sensual one moment, cool and distant the next. There is no way of forecasting which attitude will prevail at a particular time.

They tend to fall in love at first sight, and consequently learn the lessons of love the hard way – although they have very sharp and accurate intuition, which makes it unlikely that they will cultivate someone who is truly unsuitable for them. They have a short temper, and quarrel rather too easily. They express themselves hastily and over-candidly, and should take care to guard their tongues, especially when the argument is with a lover – verbal aggression comes easily to them and can do great damage.

Their metabolism has a tendency to be slow, and exercise is a useful corrective to this, although they are unlikely to relish the thought of any strenuous physical activity. They should find a way to make exercise enjoyable – they may enjoy work-outs, provided that these are oriented towards dance. Racquet sports such as tennis, badminton, or squash are popular with them.

♏ MARS IN SCORPIO

MARS USED TO rule Scorpio before the discovery of Pluto: it works strongly from this sign, and will be an influential force in the horoscope. A degree of passion is likely to sharpen the somewhat smouldering emotion of Scorpio, and these individuals need to be able to express themselves sexually with a partner who can offer equal enthusiasm and ardour. Any partnership that is not sexually fulfilled will eventually be spoiled by exasperation and resentfulness. Jealousy can become a problem, and if affronted these people will find it difficult to forgive or forget: they may even become obsessed with the offence and the person who committed it.

However, in other respects this is an excellent placing for Mars. Individuals with this placing make brilliant engineers, miners, and professionals in the wine trades. Whatever they do, they must be emotionally involved in their career; making money is enjoyable, but psychological satisfaction is more important. They may well be rather too fond of good food and drink. If this enthusiasm seems obsessive, it will be worth considering whether they are compensating for some deficiency in their emotional life. They can be secretive, and, if they do have any problems, even close friends will have difficulty discovering the truth.

The physical energy of Mars combined with the determination of Scorpio means that these people will enjoy strenuous exercise, and they are likely to excel in competitive sports.

♐ MARS IN SAGITTARIUS

RESTLESSNESS, IN one form or another, is the characteristic most clearly marked in an individual with Mars in Sagittarius in their birth chart. This can be exacerbated if they do not cultivate some form of sport or exercise that will help to diminish the very high level of physical energy that this placing of Mars confers. If this energy is not positively employed, restlessness is likely to ensue. They should find a way of balancing their physical and mental energy, using each equally.

They should ideally seek a career that is intellectually or physically demanding. They devour challenges with enthusiasm and appetite, and, faced with what others find an intractable problem, will set out their solution with enviable zeal – a solution that will probably be unconventional, ingenious, and surprising, stemming from their considerable breadth of vision.

There is a risk that in the middle of bringing their plans to fruition, restlessness will take a hand. After all their dedication and enthusiasm have been focused on one thing, they will suddenly become bored and start another project. This is because they have a tendency to believe that the grass is always greener on the other side of the fence. They should be aware of this element within their personalities, and endeavour to keep their energies focused on one thing at a time and to complete all tasks that they undertake.

These people enjoy physical risks, and will partake in sports such as rock-climbing and skiing. They are often enthusiastic gamblers.

Ptolemy's Maps
The Egyptian astronomer Ptolemy drew these celestial maps around 150 AD. He believed that the Sun, Moon, and stars revolved around the Earth.

♑ MARS IN CAPRICORN

MARS IN CAPRICORN will heighten an individual's ambition, and help spur him or her on to personal goals. This configuration also bestows great physical energy and stamina – here are natural marathon runners or long-distance swimmers, rock-climbers, and mountaineers.

These people tend to have natural ambition, and an intense will to win that is likely to be expressed in their career as well as in sport. Motivated towards success, they enjoy power, and once they have reached the top of their particular "mountain", no one is going to knock them off it. Their ambition can be so pervasive that they may neglect family and loved ones, and personal relationships may suffer. This is particularly likely if Mars receives negative aspects from Uranus, when the desire – even need – for power will be rampant. The health risk springing from this kind of attitude to life is exhaustion through over-work, so these individuals must allow themselves time to relax.

From Capricorn, Mars also brings a solid realism: these people are good to have around when there is danger – they rarely make rash judgements or silly mistakes. This is also true with relationships – they always consider carefully before making a first move. People with Mars in Capricorn can be plagued by chills and feverish complaints stemming from a sensitivity to changes of temperature.

♒ MARS IN AQUARIUS

MARS TENDS TO encourage people to be independent, and when this planet's influence is combined with that of Aquarius the need for freedom will be paramount.

Unconventionality and eccentricity will probably be marked, and even though close friends and family will be entertained by this zaniness, they will often find it embarrassing.

People with Mars in Aquarius find it difficult to use their energy evenly: they work with great bursts of enthusiasm, then quite suddenly give up, unable to summon the energy to go on. Although they wish

Aries' Ruling Planet
This 17th-century Persian illustration shows Aries symbolized by the Ram. Aries is ruled by the planet Mars.

to carry on, emotional or physical exhaustion make it feel almost impossible. Tension or stress may be at the root of the problem, and it is important for the astrologer to look at the aspects in the chart received by Mars: if the planet is afflicted by the Moon, Saturn, or Uranus, the chance of nervous strain or tension is considerable. If the individual experiences this, he or she should look for a way of releasing it such as a sporting activity or, in contrast, a relaxing technique such as yoga.

The pioneering spirit of Mars combines favourably with the humanitarian aspects of Aquarius. These people are prepared to relieve suffering at considerable hardship to themselves – they may even volunteer to help victims of famine or flood. Emotional relationships may suffer from the individual's great need for freedom. While they will enjoy sex, and may want to experiment, there is likely to be some hesitation before a permanent relationship is formed.

♓ MARS IN PISCES

THOSE PEOPLE who are born when Mars is in Pisces have an emotional force that is so strong that confining it is a danger, and failing to use it a waste. If not used positively, all this emotion can result in mental stagnation and even psychological problems.

They are perhaps most usefully occupied in the caring professions, or helping those in need, but they should also try to satisfy their own needs. They are passionate and sensual, yet they are capable of sacrificing a fulfilling personal relationship in order to pursue a vocation helping others who are in need. This placing of Mars requires other planetary influences to give practical ability and discipline, and if Mars is afflicted by Neptune, there could be indecison and a real tendency not to face up to reality.

Mars in Pisces often bestows an original imagination that will need a creative outlet, but these individuals can also be afflicted by a lack of self-confidence and they must have a great deal of reassurance and support from their friends, who will need to encourage them to follow their hearts and their instincts.

Physically, these people may not be particularly strong, and rigorous exercise is unlikely to be suitable for them, but they can make excellent skaters or dancers – skills in which their imagination and sensitivity can be lyrically expressed.

Mars glyph

PLANETS

SUN

MOON

MERCURY

VENUS

MARS

JUPITER

SATURN

URANUS

NEPTUNE

PLUTO

SIGNS

ARIES

TAURUS

GEMINI

CANCER

LEO

VIRGO

LIBRA

SCORPIO

SAGITTARIUS

CAPRICORN

AQUARIUS

PISCES

PLANETS

SUN

MOON

MERCURY

VENUS

MARS

JUPITER

SATURN

URANUS

NEPTUNE

PLUTO

SIGNS

ARIES

TAURUS

GEMINI

CANCER

LEO

VIRGO

LIBRA

SCORPIO

SAGITTARIUS

CAPRICORN

AQUARIUS

PISCES

JUPITER THROUGH THE SIGNS

The largest planet of the solar system, Jupiter takes about twelve years to travel round the Sun and through all twelve signs of the zodiac. It is connected with physical and intellectual expansion, and is associated with the acquisition of knowledge; it helps us develop a philosophical outlook, and encourages our understanding of foreign countries and people. Those with Jupiter strongly placed will, according to its sign, be optimistic and broad-minded, and direct mental energies positively. Jupiter's negative influence can cause exaggeration, extravagance, and unfounded optimism.

JUPITER IN ARIES

POSITIVE, enthusiastic Aries and adventurous, extrovert Jupiter – this combination of sign and planet has a wealth of constructive features. Those with Jupiter in Aries will be broad-minded and assertive. They are likely to possess a devil-may-care attitude, and a love of freedom that is very important to them. This must be controlled if they are not to seem inconsiderate to their partner or friends. They will be decisive, even to the point of acting more quickly than is prudent, and sometimes extravagantly generous, but they cannot resist emphasizing their own achievements and occasionally appear boastful and vainglorious – an emphasis on Virgo in their birth chart may have a steadying effect.

People with Jupiter in Aries love to travel and enjoy sport and competition, but they also have great intellectual potential, and should endeavour to develop this as they get older. As children they may need monitoring because their extroversion can lead to bullying.

JUPITER IN TAURUS

THIS PLACING of Jupiter can bring material success by encouraging an individual's desire to be successful: making money will always be a prime motive. People with Jupiter in

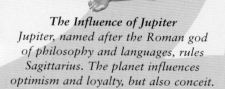

The Influence of Jupiter
Jupiter, named after the Roman god of philosophy and languages, rules Sagittarius. The planet influences optimism and loyalty, but also conceit.

Taurus usually invest cleverly and well. They have an excellent sense of timing, and are able to predict the movements of the market.

These subjects are generous, and derive great pleasure from entertaining others. This marries rather too well with one of the main attributes of this combination of planet and sign: the enjoyment of good food. These people are true gourmets and love eating and drinking, and there is a distinct possibility that under any anxiety or stress, particularly emotional stress, comfort eating becomes a problem. If Jupiter is afflicted by the Sun, Moon, or Neptune, there really will be trouble, for they are likely to become over-indulgent and greedy.

They should bear in mind that the basic principle of Jupiter is expansion, and in this case it can literally mean putting on weight!

These problems apart, people with Jupiter in Taurus make marvellous hosts, for Jupiter is at its most genial in this sign, and contributes sincerity and an excellent sense of humour. Reliable in a crisis, they have great common sense that serves them well in difficulties, and enables them to advise others equally well.

JUPITER IN GEMINI

THOSE WITH JUPITER in Gemini will be clever and versatile – perhaps too versatile for their own good, especially when they are at school, where they may be intellectually restless and disinclined to follow a single line of study. Their threshold of boredom is excessively low – boredom is a great enemy, and for that reason they sometimes find it difficult to persevere with work that requires sustained concentration.

These individuals are often clever, but tend to scatter their interests too wide, their minds ending up full of fascinating but useless information. They excel in careers that require a comprehensive general knowledge such as journalism or research, but are less likely to succeed in jobs that require single-minded study. They need to be encouraged to recognize that there is merit in the thorough knowledge of a subject. In the event of an argument, they will eventually be caught out by those who have studied the subject in question and have a real command of detail.

These individuals are tolerant and broad-minded, and tend to be abreast of contemporary thought and fashion. They are also shrewd, but indiscretion can be a problem.

JUPITER IN CANCER

JUPITER WORKS well in Cancer, and people with this placing love their home and their family, but are also devoted to humanitarian action in general. They have a wonderful natural sympathy and kindness, and an instinctive understanding of others' problems and difficulties. They will be the first to reach for their wallet or credit card when reports of mass starvation come to their attention, and on a personal level they often show their concern by working in the caring professions.

If there is creative ability shown elsewhere in the chart, this placing of Jupiter will certainly enhance it since the imagination will combine with Cancerian intuition. But these people tend to be unsure in their opinions, and this is often shown in a tendency to move from one area of work to another, or to change political or religious commitments.

They are as devoted to family life as they are to their humanitarian work, and there can be difficulties when one comes into conflict with the other – if only in the amount of time available for each. They will be very eager for their children to have a range of interests equal to their own, and will do everything possible to broaden and develop their child's experience and intelligence.

People with Jupiter in Cancer are very shrewd in business, and are likely to make a success of any enterprise that they undertake. They may also do well in the antique trade because they enjoy building up a detailed knowledge of a particular period of history or area of art.

JUPITER IN LEO

JUPITER STANDS centre stage when it is in Leo, and so will people with this placing of the planet: they will possess great dramatic flair, and any accusation of showiness will probably be well founded. They often have a right to be proud, for they have qualities that deserve to be recognized, such as intelligence, ambition, and acting ability.

However, the danger of over-doing things is very considerable indeed. These are people whose passion for life, and for making the fullest possible use of every moment, is in itself excellent, but can be extremely wearing. They should curb their inflated egos and avoid self-satisfaction and bombast, allowing their natural enthusiasm to inspire others rather than trying to dragoon them into enthusiasm or action. They should be careful not to become figures of fun in their enjoyment of sometimes unusual or over-showy clothing. Pomposity can be one of their less attractive traits, and they are advised to take note of anyone who suggests that they are beginning to err in that respect. All

this will be exacerbated if the Sun makes a negative aspect to Jupiter. Despite these potential problems, this can be a valuable placing of Jupiter, especially for those involved in challenging intellectual projects in which they will excel. Any natural creative flair will also be enhanced.

JUPITER IN VIRGO

JUPITER ENCOURAGES expansion and the broad approach to life; Virgo favours a narrower, more detailed approach. There can be conflict when the individual is faced with the need to take a broad view of a situation, for in attempting to do so, he or she may unexpectedly lose self-confidence and be unable to make a firm decision. Fortunately, Jupiter brings from Virgo a matter-of-fact approach to life, which will help individuals reach the right conclusions, and as time goes on they will be able to look back on a number of successes, the recollection of which will bolster their faith in themselves and their judgement.

If Jupiter is afflicted by either the Moon or Mercury, these people can be absent-minded. This will infuriate them, and they need to avoid the consequences by making notes and arranging reminders to themselves.

This position of Jupiter occurs in the horoscopes of a number of notable writers because the patience and total dedication of a meticulous craftsperson is combined with the intelligence to express a highly vivid imaginative talent. The subject will also possess healthy scepticism and critical acumen. Jupiter in Virgo bestows a practical flair, and is a fine attribute in the horoscope of a scientist or technician, or anyone involved in technology.

Healthwise, there may be digestive problems or constipation, especially if there is a love of rich food.

The Archer
Sagittarius, depicted here in a Turkish manuscript of the 16th century, is symbolized by the Archer.

PLANETS
SUN
MOON
MERCURY
VENUS
MARS
JUPITER
SATURN
URANUS
NEPTUNE
PLUTO

SIGNS
ARIES
TAURUS
GEMINI
CANCER
LEO
VIRGO
LIBRA
SCORPIO
SAGITTARIUS
CAPRICORN
AQUARIUS
PISCES

PLANETS

SUN

MOON

MERCURY

VENUS

MARS

JUPITER

SATURN

URANUS

NEPTUNE

PLUTO

SIGNS

ARIES

TAURUS

GEMINI

CANCER

LEO

VIRGO

LIBRA

SCORPIO

SAGITTARIUS

CAPRICORN

AQUARIUS

PISCES

JUPITER IN LIBRA

THIS PLACING reveals an easy-going, casual, sympathetic, kindly, and completely charming person who loves comfort. If Jupiter receives a negative aspect from Venus, these qualities will be exaggerated and the person can become indolent and lazy, although still utterly charming, and capable of using that charm in order to contrive a luxurious lifestyle that will be supported by the hard work of others.

However, these people have good minds under normal circumstances, and are capable of using them. They may be driven to uncharacteristic hard work by their need to make money in order to enjoy the comfortable, even luxurious, lifestyle that they require if they are to be happy. The comfort and luxury they attain will be shared generously, even extravagantly, with friends, and a person with Jupiter in Libra usually has a well-deserved reputation as a genial host.

The love of entertainment felt by those with Jupiter in Libra stems partially from their hatred of loneliness, and they will cultivate both business and emotional partnerships. These individuals give a great deal of love and affection to partners, but they are not very independent, and often rely heavily on others. They need encouragment to develop their own potential and to stand alone. They often dislike exercise but should endeavour to be active, not only for their health and well-being, but because they enjoy rich food and need to work off the excess calories.

JUPITER IN SCORPIO

IF JUPITER IS well aspected in a birth chart, the subject will live life to the full, and be emotionally absorbed in everything he or she does. Subjects are likely to be enterprising and determined to fulfil their potential. If Jupiter is also in Scorpio, they will possess great staying-power and motivation, assets that will help them to achieve all of their ambitions.

Scorpio is not a sign that will tolerate half-measures, and Jupiter at its strongest is equally resolute. These two influences combine to create a character who has a desire for progress in every area of life. These individuals want to feel they are moving forward, to see natural development taking place, whether in their career or their emotional life. Action is their byword, and too often they seem not to have heard of moderation. These people have a tendency to overdo things and can burn themselves out in their pursuit of business and pleasure. They need to pace themselves, but may find this difficult, especially if

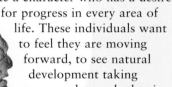

Zeus and Jupiter
The Greeks' parallel god to Jupiter was Zeus. This statue is a Hellenistic copy of a 4th-century BC statue of Jupiter.

the Sun or Moon squares or opposes Jupiter, when there will be a danger of mental strain. Another problem is their natural capacity for suspicion, which they must control if it is not to become overly obsessive.

On the positive side, there is often financial aptitude and great generosity, although this can be accompanied by vanity and pride. These people also tend to have a flair for verbal aggression, which can be used most constructively if they wish to become lawyers or barristers, and they are likely to enjoy great success in these careers.

JUPITER IN SAGITTARIUS

JUPITER RULES Sagittarius and those born with Jupiter in that sign have a natural happy-go-lucky side to their character. In early life this can work against them, when they are likely to prefer the sports field to the classroom or lecture hall. They may incur sports injuries because their exuberance can lead to recklessness.

They are optimistic to a fault and admirably if indiscriminately enthusiastic; blind optimism is not unknown, especially if Jupiter is afflicted by opposition or square aspects from the Sun, Mercury, or Mars. Some steadying influence in the birth chart is desirable – check to see if Saturn is well placed or if a personal planet is in an earth sign.

Individuals with this placing will begin to develop intellectually when they are out of the first flush of youth; they will become thoughtful, even philosophical. They recognize that they always need to be learning. Here are the eternal students, whose desire is to find a subject that they can explore thoroughly, fulfilling and increasing their admirable intellectual potential. They will also possess a wonderful sense of justice, and they are likely to have a flair for languages and a love of travel.

Jupiter works very strongly from Sagittarius, therefore the traits listed in The Sun in Sagittarius (*see page 16*) will be emphasized.

Early Stargazers
From the earliest times until
the 18th century, astronomers
also studied astrology.

♑ JUPITER IN CAPRICORN

HERE ARE rather remarkable people, the product of the combination (at best, a successful blending) of very different characteristics: the positive, extroverted qualities of Jupiter, and the negative, introverted qualities of Capricorn. Individuals born with this combination of planet and sign will be ambitious and determined, welcoming responsibility, able and willing to work extremely hard and persistently, and having admirable powers of concentration. Their outlook on life will be very sensible and intelligent, and they will accept challenges realistically. The influence of Capricorn prevents the blind optimism of Jupiter, and common sense and caution will always inform their every move.

The generosity and flamboyance of Jupiter are not often seen when it is in this sign, and the subject may occasionally have a pessimistic or bleak view of life, but their quirky sense of humour is never far away.

These people are usually kind-hearted and thoughtful, although they tend to believe that they are always right, occasionally to the point of pig-headedness. This will be a real problem only if Jupiter receives a square aspect from the Sun or Moon, in which case it is likely that the individual will be so stubborn that he or she will refuse to listen to the opinion of others. When Jupiter is in Capricorn it is important also to consider the position of Saturn in the chart; if it is heavily aspected to the personal planets, Capricorn's influence can overshadow that of Jupiter's, and the subject will be sober and serious.

As children, those with Jupiter in Capricorn work cautiously, plodding slowly and deliberately up through the ranks of their contemporaries, eventually reaching the head of the class. For these individuals, making steady, gradual progress is likely to be the pattern throughout life.

♒ JUPITER IN AQUARIUS

PEOPLE WITH this placing of Jupiter will have powerful humanitarian emotions, and will put them to practical use in helping both friends and strangers. They need to help, and have the imagination and originality to do it in a rewarding and unpatronizing way.

As individuals, they are tolerant and impartial, fully sympathetic to the hardships and predicaments of others – but again, strongly practical and unsentimental. The humour of Jupiter will warm their Aquarian coolness, and it will not be difficult to become friendly with them.

Their preoccupation with helping others will not deprive them of the energetic social life they so much enjoy: they will have a wide circle of friends and acquaintances who will be roped in to help with their philanthropic work. They have an exceptionally strong sense of justice, and if unfairness or prejudice arises in any situation, they are always prepared to stand up and fight it.

Their sense of humour may strike others as eccentric, and sometimes distinctly unfunny, and if Jupiter is afflicted there is likely to be a total absence of tact, and sometimes stubborn intolerance – although this is usually directed at entirely proper targets. Intuition will be keen and dependable, and scientific ability, or literary or musical talent may be present.

♓ JUPITER IN PISCES

BEFORE THE DISCOVERY of Neptune, Jupiter ruled Pisces. As a result, it works powerfully from this sign, and is positively placed. The philosophical, spiritual, and reflective elements of sign and planet are well matched. Kindness, sympathy, and a caring attitude towards others will be marked, and compassion will be married to a natural friendliness that ensures that sympathy and help are offered in a manner that is easy to accept.

Those working in the caring professions often have this placing of Jupiter in their charts – it can be instrumental in their choice of career, and will assist them to make progress, whether as doctors, nurses, or aid workers. These people also make good vets, for they tend to have a natural love of animals and a considerable rapport with them.

Emotion, imagination, and intuition are all enhanced by Jupiter working from Pisces, and religious individuals are likely to practise what they preach, often identifying with less favoured people in the community, whose sufferings they will feel impelled to alleviate. In some individuals, their desire to help is expressed through meditation – in a contemplative religious order, for instance – while some are natural healers of the body and mind.

If Jupiter is afflicted by the Sun or Moon, there are likely to be elements of self-indulgence in the personality, as well as a tendency towards self-deception and deceptiveness.

Jupiter glyph

PLANETS

SUN
MOON
MERCURY
VENUS
MARS
JUPITER
SATURN
URANUS
NEPTUNE
PLUTO

SIGNS

ARIES
TAURUS
GEMINI
CANCER
LEO
VIRGO
LIBRA
SCORPIO
SAGITTARIUS
CAPRICORN
AQUARIUS
PISCES

SATURN THROUGH THE SIGNS

Saturn takes twenty-nine years to complete one cycle of the zodiac. It represents responsibility and discipline, and the sign in which it appears will reveal where a person must learn lessons in life, and also in what areas limitations might be found. Saturn is often our inner voice of caution and reason, and in the process of learning when to listen to this voice and when to disobey, we will either gain self-confidence because we have taken a prudent and successful line of action, or regress because we have been rash. Through Saturn we can develop discipline, discrimination, and patience.

SATURN IN ARIES

THE FORCES attributed to this planet and sign are very different: Saturn bestows caution and restriction, while Aries is associated with vigour and energy. These very contrasting factors cause conflict in the personalities of subjects born when Saturn was in Aries. Sometimes they will be strong, assertive, and courageous, at other times hesitant and unable to decide on the right course of action.

If they are able to achieve a balance between the two sides of their personality, they can combine these apparently contradictory traits in the most advantageous manner, so that extremes of action and inaction are avoided. Arien strength and vigour can be tempered by Saturnian practicality and common sense, while Saturnian ambition will be boosted by Arien energy. Persistence and determination are not completely curbed, but physical and emotional energy is tempered.

These people often feel restless when the pace of life slows down, and they have a tendency to submit to depression. The best antidote to this is a change of occupation, or a vigorous exercise or sport to work off their excessive energy.

Saturn in Aries can also cause these individuals to be self-centred and thoughtless, and sometimes they will have difficulty communicating and co-operating with others.

The Influence of Saturn
Saturn, named after an agricultural god, rules Capricorn. Saturn influences caution and practicality, but also limitation and narrow-mindedness.

SATURN IN TAURUS

TAUREAN PATIENCE complements Saturn's caution, and people born with this combination of planet and sign in the birth chart will tend to be long-suffering, hard-working, and follow a prudent and rather rigid routine throughout their life. Their admirable patience and discretion sometimes seem to sap them of enthusiasm and originality.

Saturn's ambition will spur these individuals on to the top of their professions, but there can sometimes be a conflict between the Taurean love of luxury and the Saturnian need to be "careful" with money. They usually have an inner voice that accuses them of spending too lavishly, or living too well. They will have to learn to ignore this voice sometimes, if they wish to indulge their Taurean instincts.

Although kindly to others, these subjects are inhibited when expressing their emotions in a personal relationship. Their caution and patience tends to become hesitancy and indecision, and parents with this placing find themselves alternately over-strict with and indulgent to their children. Consider the horoscope in its entirety to see if these contrasting traits will be easy to reconcile. If extroverted tendencies are found elsewhere in the chart, they can weaken the Saturnian influence and lighten the character.

SATURN IN GEMINI

SATURN'S EFFECT from Gemini is generally positive because it stabilizes the personality and ensures that the intellect is focused. These people will be more economical with words than other Geminis, and will put their views across forcefully, succinctly, and impartially. They are capable of highly disciplined thought, and often excel at mathematics and science.

However, they are quite often considered uncommunicative, and when they do speak out they are likely to be cynical or sarcastic. They often have to resort to their off-beat Saturnian humour when they offend others by expressing themselves more harshly than they intended. They insist on honesty in communication, but they need to guard against excessive criticism.

These individuals are prone to suspicion and doubt, and positive thinking and an optimistic outlook should be cultivated if not found elsewhere in the chart. Look at the positions of Mercury and Jupiter to see if their influences might help.

SATURN IN CANCER

A CONSIDERABLE degree of financial shrewdness is possessed by those with Saturn in Cancer, and these subjects will have not only the ability to make money but also the intuition to invest it advantageously. They also possess a strong sense of purpose, and great tenacity when following a decided course.

The need for real emotional stability is very strong, but the ease or difficulty with which this is achieved will often depend on how the individual was treated as a child. If the father was particularly strict, for instance, or there was some kind of emotional deprivation, the person may have suffered and, as a result, may find it difficult to take even small problems in his or her stride.

Saturn in Cancer often indicates someone who has a great desire for a stable and secure family life but has problems achieving it. These people have a tendency towards anxiety, but find it difficult to share their problems with others. If this is not to affect their relationships, and make them inhibited with their partners, they must try their best to free their emotions. If Mars or Jupiter is placed in a fire sign, or if either is well aspected, this can do much to alleviate the problem.

SATURN IN LEO

PEOPLE BORN when Saturn was in Leo will take life seriously, and the warmer, fiery qualities of Leo will

tend not to burn as brightly as they could, unless there are other planets also occupying this sign. Even then, Saturn will cloud a Leonine Sun. These people possess strength of will, loyalty, determination, and excellent organizing ability, and they have the ability to cope with the most difficult situation decisively and competently. However, they are often guilty of autocracy and pride.

They are unwilling to accept any limitation, and need to attain the goals they set themselves. Prepared to impose any discipline they feel is necessary to get to the top, once they have set themselves a goal, they pursue it to the exclusion of all else. This not only deprives them of a great deal of pleasure, but can harm their personal relationships with those less concerned with ambition and achievement. They tend to lose their sense of perspective, and often their loyalty can be misplaced, too.

These people seem to have an inner voice that is harsh and over-authoritative. Even when they know that a gentle, sympathetic approach would suit their needs, they seem to choose the most painful course of action. Their habit of rigid self-discipline may be the result of an austere and conventional childhood, and parents with Saturn in Leo can be autocratic and severe.

To improve their relationships, the subjects must learn to suppress their desire for power and develop objective values and opinions. They should try to satisfy others' needs as well as their own.

Capricorn
Saturn rules Capricorn, the tenth sign of the zodiac, and bestows ambition, the need to do the right and proper thing, and a love of tradition. This illustration is from the Bedford Hours, *1423.*

SATURN IN VIRGO

WHEN SATURN IS in Virgo, it attempts to impose a very strict adherence to routine and encourages caution, prudence, patience, and modesty. Together with a strong sense of duty, these qualities will help individuals to work methodically and often successfully in any occupation.

Their own rigid attitude to work can make them expect too much of less meticulous people, and when subjects with Saturn in Virgo are given authority over others, the regime they impose can be rather too austere and demanding, often alienating colleagues. Adherence to discipline, a powerful critical sense, and the aim to perform every task perfectly are admirable qualities, but need to be accompanied with sensitivity and thoughtfulness when brought to bear on others.

Too often these people sound sarcastic and carping, but this also applies to their inner voice too. Seeing themselves as failing to achieve perfection, they can become self-critical and lose confidence in their own abilities – this can affect their dealings with those around them, but more importantly, they become introverted and shy. Learning to use Saturn in Virgo as a strong anchor, the practical caution it offers will be of the greatest help. It is well worth watching out for signs of obsession, which can build up under stress.

PLANETS

SUN

MOON

MERCURY

VENUS

MARS

JUPITER

SATURN

URANUS

NEPTUNE

PLUTO

SIGNS

ARIES

TAURUS

GEMINI

CANCER

LEO

VIRGO

LIBRA

SCORPIO

SAGITTARIUS

CAPRICORN

AQUARIUS

PISCES

PLANETS
SUN
MOON
MERCURY
VENUS
MARS
JUPITER
SATURN
URANUS
NEPTUNE
PLUTO
SIGNS
ARIES
TAURUS
GEMINI
CANCER
LEO
VIRGO
LIBRA
SCORPIO
SAGITTARIUS
CAPRICORN
AQUARIUS
PISCES

SATURN IN LIBRA

SATURN IS TRADITIONALLY "well placed" in Libra, and indeed the qualities of the planet and the sign seem to have a strong affinity. Individuals born with this placing have a natural sense of justice, and powerful empathy with those who have been unfairly treated. They are impartial, flexible, and fair, and positively need to see justice done. Kindness is directed by common sense, and advice will always be offered tactfully and diplomatically.

These people need a permanent emotional relationship, but often seem to go out of their way to avoid one, usually because they find it difficult to express their emotions freely. Occasionally there is deep-seated sexual inhibition. They may offer convincing practical excuses for not committing themselves, but one can usually be sure that the real reason lies much deeper than the excuse offered. Saturn in this position will sharpen the conscience, and when Libra prompts resentment at some supposed lack of gratitude in a friend, Saturn intervenes and

does much to soften the bitterness that can be expressed. If Saturn receives any negative aspects, or makes a square or opposition to the Ascendant, intolerance may be shown towards partner or colleagues, especially if Saturn is in the seventh or tenth house. If it is in the fourth house, there may be discontent with the domestic situation, or perhaps a desire to move home frequently. Particular attention must always be shown to Saturn's house position.

SATURN IN SCORPIO

EVEN WHEN THE horoscope as a whole is positive, extroverted, and lively, Saturn will shed a somewhat baleful light from Scorpio. The subject will have a dark, brooding intensity, although his or her rather dour personality is usually lightened by an off-beat sense of humour. People with this position of Saturn will be purposeful and determined, with a great deal of emotional energy directed at achieving their objectives. They will also have an exceptionally shrewd business sense, and usually do very well indeed in big business or on the international money market. Hard work and a strong emotional commitment to the objective goes without saying, but Scorpio can often over-rule Saturnian caution, and then there will be a strong tendency to over-spend.

The Harvester
Saturn was once the god of the seasons and agriculture – which is why he carries a sickle. He presided over the Roman Saturnalia, a festival that later became Christmas.

People with a powerful Scorpio influence know how to enjoy themselves, and are willing to spend money on good food and wine. The position of Jupiter and Venus in a horoscope will show how strong the sybaritic tendency is likely to be.

On the negative side, obsessive tendencies are all too likely, with perseverance becoming fixation and stubbornness. There can also be a somewhat cruel streak, emerging when the subject is striving for a goal and finds others standing in the way. Ruthlessness can then surface.

This position of Saturn can complicate the sex life by inhibiting a full expression of desire, and making the subject feel restless and unfulfilled. In a partnership, the inner voice sometimes instigates jealousy, and if this is not combated it can have a negative effect, not only on a partnership but on the subject's own equilibrium – and sometimes on the physical well-being.

SATURN IN SAGITTARIUS

JUPITER, THE RULER of Sagittarius, is essentially the polar planet to Saturn, the former representing expansion and the latter restriction. Although this may seem a poor position for Saturn, there are in fact some benefits. Saturn shining from Sagittarius strengthens the person's capacity for concentration and encourages study; those with this combination of sign and planet have no difficulty in fulfilling their intellectual potential. Young children with this placing often appear to have "an old head on young shoulders", and they are the kind of people whom reincarnationists speak of as "old souls".

As both children and adults, these individuals are straightforward and honest, particularly in speech. They will not hesitate to utter truths that may be out of line with the conventional view of things. When faced with a challenge, however, they can be less brave. They want to act as positively as they speak,

PLANETS

SUN

MOON

MERCURY

VENUS

MARS

JUPITER

SATURN

URANUS

NEPTUNE

PLUTO

SIGNS

ARIES

TAURUS

GEMINI

CANCER

LEO

VIRGO

LIBRA

SCORPIO

SAGITTARIUS

CAPRICORN

AQUARIUS

PISCES

but Saturn's influence dampens the self-confidence and enthusiasm of Sagittarius, and this can result in the inhibition of endeavour. This caution can sometimes amount to trepidation, which is likely to stand in the way of accomplishment.

If aspects to Saturn are positive, and if there is a lot of fire and air in the horoscope, the chances are that inhibition will be minimal. If the birth chart shows someone shy and sensitive, however, an inner voice may have a strongly inhibitive effect on the subject's actions.

SATURN IN CAPRICORN

SATURN RULES CAPRICORN, therefore the planet works powerfully from this sign. People with this placing possess determination, ambition, and practical ability, excellently controlled by a measure of caution.

These individuals may make too many sacrifices in order to achieve personal ambitions, and this can have a detrimental effect on their family life, with too much time spent at work and too little time at home. This is not because they care too little for their partner or children, but paradoxically because they care too much, and are eager to provide well for them. The strong materialistic streak that often runs through the character of these subjects makes it very difficult for them to achieve a balance between home and work.

If Saturn is negatively aspected, the outlook can be pessimistic and sombre. However, people with this placing of Saturn seem to enjoy being faced with difficulties, and will "grin and bear it". They often yearn for power, which is often of a political nature, and they show the Capricornian proclivity for social climbing. If Saturn is afflicted it can indicate parsimony, but on the whole the positive aspects of this placing should dominate.

Exercise is important because Saturn rules the bones, and stiffness in the joints should be prevented.

The Teacher
Saturn, the god, is often portrayed as a wise old man. In astrology he is seen as the teacher.

SATURN IN AQUARIUS

SATURN RULED AQUARIUS before the discovery of Uranus, and while its power from this sign may not equal its strength when in Capricorn, it still works powerfully here, and its effect is generally very positive.

It gives the subject determination to pursue his or her ambitions, and a strongly original mind. Scientific potential will be encouraged by Saturn from this sign, and so will the Aquarian humanitarian impulse.

There is a tendency for early opinions to become fixed, and if ideas or opinions are contested these people can be stubborn, and resort to cunning to achieve their goals.

Those with Saturn in Aquarius are often torn between a desire for convention and the inclination to be unconventional. Subjects will alternately need safety and security, then adventure, originality, and independence. A painful conflict can arise when they find it difficult to throw away all their carefully laid plans in order to act on impulse.

These people are generally friendly, but sometimes the Aquarian need for privacy will arise, and even though it brings loneliness they will shrink away from close contact with others. The influence of the Sun, Moon, and Ascendant in the birth chart, may help resolve the inherent conflicts that exist in this placing.

SATURN IN PISCES

SHYNESS AND INHIBITION can all too often make life difficult for those with Saturn in Pisces. The planet brings wholly admirable qualities from this sign: humility, sympathy, and the capacity for self-sacrifice, but although intuition will be strong and dependable, there is not usually a great deal of self-confidence, and the instinct to shrink from action can prevent these people from making any real progress.

The attractive side of this picture shows self-effacing individuals, who are continually failing to recognize their own real value to society and their friends. Hopefully, influences will be found elsewhere in these people's horoscopes that will give them the strength to counter their negative tendencies. Saturn in Pisces should be disabling only if the rest of the birth chart indicates a rather pessimistic outlook on life.

To gain confidence and find their true potential, these people need to tap into the powerful imaginative force that Saturn brings them from Pisces. Look elsewhere in the birth chart for suggestions as to how this may be achieved – perhaps through writing or another creative activity – but they are likely to need a lot of encouragement to persevere.

There is the possibility of quick changes of mood, and a tendency to worry (exacerbated if Saturn receives negative aspects from the Moon) that can sometimes lead to hypochondria.

Saturn glyph

PLANETS

SUN

MOON

MERCURY

VENUS

MARS

JUPITER

SATURN

URANUS

NEPTUNE

PLUTO

SIGNS

ARIES

TAURUS

GEMINI

CANCER

LEO

VIRGO

LIBRA

SCORPIO

SAGITTARIUS

CAPRICORN

AQUARIUS

PISCES

URANUS THROUGH THE SIGNS

Uranus is the first of the "modern" planets. Its sign position will reveal the way in which a person's need for individuality is expressed. The planet takes approximately seven years to pass through each sign of the zodiac, therefore it will be in the same sign in the horoscope of everyone born in that seven-year period. Consequently, the sign in which Uranus falls, like Neptune and Pluto, indicates generational differences. Its sign position will not be as important as its house position in a birth chart, and its influence will not be as personal as that of the preceding planets in this section.

URANUS IN ARIES

IN THIS position, the forthright, nervous energy of Uranus is complemented by the headstrong assertiveness of Aries, so this is an excellent and serviceable position for the planet. Aries' pioneering spirit will also be strengthened by the influence of Uranus, and there will be an interest in new and unusual projects. If there are signs of creativity elsewhere in the chart, Uranus can encourage originality and the appreciation of colour.

Self-confidence is enhanced by this placing, and the individual will have a strong sense of leadership. However, these people need to curb their proclivity for foolhardiness and rash courses of action.

From Aries, Uranus does not encourage patience, and if Uranus is afflicted, the individual may be inconsistent and unpredictable. It is worth looking at other areas of the horoscope to see if patience and caution are present elsewhere. If Mars squares or opposes Uranus, the subject is likely to be tense, nervous, and emotional.

URANUS IN TAURUS

STUBBORNNESS will be the hallmark of people who are born with Uranus in Taurus, and it will be exacerbated if other fixed signs are prominent in

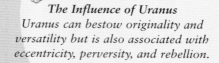

The Influence of Uranus
Uranus can bestow originality and versatility but is also associated with eccentricity, perversity, and rebellion.

the horoscope. These subjects often seem to be totally inflexible, and once they have made up their minds it is impossible to make them revise their opinion – with the possibility that even changes in social attitudes or fashion will pass them by.

This position is excellent if the horoscope in general suggests self-doubt or indecision. For instance, if there is an emphasis on Libra, Uranus will then contribute a degree of stability and firmness of purpose that might otherwise be missing.

These people may sometimes feel a clash between the Taurean desire to take a conventional view or action, and the Uranian instinct to be unconventional and suddenly do something that is surprising and distinctive. People who can balance

these two instincts tend to be original and practical, and their contributions at times of difficulty are extremely valuable – the influences of Uranus and Taurus working in combination, are at their best. These subjects may occasionally have a rather eccentric and contrary attitude to money; one minute they are over-extravagant, spending a great deal on glamorous evenings out, the next they suddenly pull in their horns and economize rigorously.

URANUS IN GEMINI

URANUS WORKS well from Gemini, where it encourages dynamism, liveliness, and originality. Those with Uranus in this sign are capable of making innovative contributions to a discussion or line of action. However, they should be encouraged to pause for a second before leaping in with their suggestions, for they tend not to think things through.

If the birth chart suggests an individual with an intellectual bent, for instance, if Mercury and Jupiter are well placed by sign and aspect, then Uranus in Gemini should be especially beneficial, sharpening the attitude and response, especially in argument and debate. Individuals who work in the media, or follow an academic or political career, are likely to benefit. The technical side of the communications industry may also appeal to these subjects.

The restless and nervous Gemini influence combined with the tension of Uranus can cause problems with stress. Study the full birth chart to see if Uranus receives oppositions or squares from the Sun, Moon, Ascendant, or Mercury. If so, such an aspect is likely to be a source of tension: individuals worry about the fact that they have difficulty in relaxing or sleeping. Relaxation techniques such as yoga may help. If Mars is badly aspected there may be a tendency to suffer from headaches.

URANUS IN CANCER

AT ITS BEST, Uranus in Cancer enhances the imagination, which will have a wonderfully original slant; it is definitely an asset in the horoscope of anyone who has creative ability. However, those born with Uranus in Cancer will often feel confused because of their urge to act idiosyncratically.

Uranus combined with the changeable moodiness of Cancer can cause problems. Uranus is a cold, unemotional planet that encourages logical thinking and clear, decisive action. Cancer, on the other hand, is associated with intuition and emotion. If Uranus is personalized, or the Sun, Moon, or Ascending sign is Cancer, inner confusion is likely to be a source of tension. This confusion affects not only the subject, but those around him or her, who never quite know where they stand, or what to expect.

Individuals with this combination should try to let the qualities of the planet and sign complement each other, rather than fight. Remember that Uranus is a generational influence, so the more powerful, personal planets will hopefully dominate and moderate its effect.

URANUS IN LEO

DYNAMIC ENERGY and the capacity for vigorous leadership are often evident when Uranus is in Leo, and people born with this combination of planet and sign tend to relish power, to the extent that they can be positively autocratic. If Uranus was in the fifth house at the time of birth, there will almost certainly be a desire to influence the masses. If they can control autocracy and personal pride, these people will be able to make a very positive contribution in their generation.

Uranus in Leo is lively and inspiriting, and the individual is likely to be charismatic. There may be a strong sense of the dramatic, helpful in public speaking, and because Leo is a creative sign there is often inventive flair.

There are one or two problems with which it is necessary to come to terms, however. Leo is a fixed sign, while Uranus is associated with stubbornness, and the individual with this blend of influences can become a completely immovable object that the most powerful force has difficulty in shifting. Leo is also a warm and enthusiastic fire sign, while Uranus is somewhat distant, and can sometimes seem cool, calculating, and unemotional.

However, this will be a problem only if Uranus is a personal planet, or negatively aspected by the Sun. In a birth chart that suggests little self-confidence, this placing can be a great help.

URANUS IN VIRGO

FROM VIRGO, Uranus will encourage the individual to work in detail, to analyze and research, and it inspires an original approach to any project. Virgo, an earth sign, tends to be very conventional, encouraging people to go for well-tried, familiar courses of action; Uranus demands originality and innovation. There may be an inner conflict between the two urges, but if there is some way that they can be reconciled, the individual can be spectacularly successful in solving problems that are too difficult for others.

Anyone with Uranus in Virgo will necessarily have Pluto in that sign, too, and many will have these two planets in conjunction, a very powerful combination because Pluto endows these subjects with dynamic, forceful qualities, and makes them capable of drastic action and change when it is necessary. These people will query everything. They are unlikely to accept official answers to any large question, and are always eager to get to the truth.

Individuals who have Uranus in Virgo tend to scrutinize every aspect of a situation, and this proclivity will be valuable if the person wishes to pursue investigative or research work, particularly in medicine. A flair for science is also possible.

These people must learn to reconcile the different elements of their personality and accept Uranus' encouragement to be "different"; it would be unfortunate to allow the Virgoan side of their character to suppress their originality.

New Ruler
Uranus has ruled Aquarius since its discovery in 1781, but at the time of this 17th-century Persian illustration, Aquarius was ruled by Saturn.

SUN

MOON

MERCURY

VENUS

MARS

JUPITER

SATURN

URANUS

NEPTUNE

PLUTO

SIGNS

ARIES

TAURUS

GEMINI

CANCER

LEO

VIRGO

LIBRA

SCORPIO

SAGITTARIUS

CAPRICORN

AQUARIUS

PISCES

PLANETS

SUN

MOON

MERCURY

VENUS

MARS

JUPITER

SATURN

URANUS

NEPTUNE

PLUTO

SIGNS

ARIES

TAURUS

GEMINI

CANCER

LEO

VIRGO

LIBRA

SCORPIO

SAGITTARIUS

CAPRICORN

AQUARIUS

PISCES

♎ URANUS IN LIBRA

FROM LIBRA, Uranus can contribute great powers of attraction, similar to those found in a Sun-sign Libran. The subjects are often loving and romantic, but unlike Sun-sign Librans, they will possess a strong independent streak from Uranus that will battle constantly against their Libran longing for a solid and lasting personal relationship. The partner of a person with Uranus in Libra will sometimes feel that he or she is being treated coolly, and that his or her lover is too independent to make a proper commitment.

In most cases, only a thread of independence will emerge in the attitude towards partners, but if either Venus or Uranus is a personal planet, or they are in aspect to each other, these contrasting traits – desire for both partnership and independence – may cause problems in a relationship. If Aquarius is the Sun, Moon, or Ascendant, it is likely that this person wants a partnership, but not a particular partner. It is important for such individuals to come to terms with this facet of their personality if they are to be honest with potential partners.

People with Uranus in Libra make faithful friends who are completely dependable, and always ready to give as much consideration and time to their friends as they need. Sympathy and kindness are attributes that Uranus certainly

encourages from Libra. Those who are accused of being a little too cool and distant to relatives and loved ones should try to cultivate the same degree of affection they show their friends.

This combination of planet and sign is excellent for people with a very high emotional level, for it will help to stabilize and rationalize their approach and reaction to life in general.

♏ URANUS IN SCORPIO

THE INFLUENCE of Uranus is at its most intricate when working from Scorpio. The planet is exalted in this sign, so its strength will be increased dramatically. When its dynamic force is added to the emotional intensity of Scorpio, it will endow these individuals with extraordinary power. They will be brave and daring but tend to disguise this fact. They do not like to show emotion or lose control, and will always remain calm on the surface even if inwardly they are boiling with anger or disgust. It is very important for these subjects to use their emotions constructively – and for them to release them gradually so that positive achievements and inner satisfaction might be gained.

Uranus was in Scorpio from 1975 to 1981, and those born during this period are still quite young. The most dynamic of this generation will have either a Sun or a Moon

in Scorpio, or a Scorpio Ascendant. They will feel a powerful need to influence the course of world events and many of them do so, sometimes by the most positive and telling arguments and actions, sometimes by behaviour that is quite negative and destructive. Parents who have children with Uranus in Scorpio in their chart should try to help them recognize and avoid their tendency to feel depressed about problems such as poverty and environmental pollution, because this despair can turn to negative thinking and self-destructive behaviour.

♐ URANUS IN SAGITTARIUS

SAGITTARIUS IS a lively, dynamic placing for this sometimes rather equivocal planet – one that gives a very original slant to the intellect and opens up the mind. There will be a strong Sagittarian need for challenge that is complemented by an attraction to all new and original things. These individuals are often attracted towards the most up-to-date developments in technology.

It will not be surprising to find Uranus in Sagittarius in the horoscopes of those particularly concerned with ecology and the problems of the environment. Working in this field will enable these individuals to express their originality and mental vigour. Both intellectually and physically adventurous, they will be quick to use their talents in the most positive way, possibly employing science to prevent future ecological disasters.

Their approach to the problems of the Earth will be very different from those with Uranus in Scorpio: they are unlikely to possess the latter's tendency towards negative thinking, and, provided they are encouraged as children to recognize the beauty of the Earth, they will grow up with a deeply protective attitude towards it. These traits should be strongly pronounced and highly powerful if Sagittarius is prominent or if Uranus is personalized in the birth chart.

The Water-bearer Aquarius is symbolized by the water-bearer, who spills out life-force and spiritual energy to mankind.

PLANETS

SUN

MOON

MERCURY

VENUS

MARS

JUPITER

SATURN

URANUS

NEPTUNE

PLUTO

SIGNS

ARIES

TAURUS

GEMINI

CANCER

LEO

VIRGO

LIBRA

SCORPIO

SAGITTARIUS

CAPRICORN

AQUARIUS

PISCES

♑ URANUS IN CAPRICORN

A CERTAIN AMOUNT of conflict will be the result of Uranus in the sign of Capricorn, for the planet often encourages unexpected and original responses, including unpredictability to the point of perversity, while the sign is one of rationality, coolness of outlook, and the ability to put problems in the most coherent and logical perspective.

Some individuals will find these conflicting attitudes confusing, and will have difficulty in deciding how to overcome particular problems. However, those who are able to use the two conflicting approaches to weigh up situations with clear-headed reason, and then act, often unexpectedly and with original flair, will get the best of two worlds. Remember that Uranus' effect is on a whole generation of people, and that while these traits will not be strong in everyone born during the seven years when Uranus is in Capricorn, the flavour of originality married to logic will be present in the personality to some degree.

The humanitarian side of Uranus will be apparent in these people, and it will be put to work in a practical and down-to-earth way. However, because they are capable of being cruel to be kind, their solutions can sometimes appear rather harsh.

Look at the rest of the subject's birth chart to see if the power of Uranus is strong elsewhere. If so, it is possible that the person will lead that generation. You should also refer to both Saturn and Neptune in Capricorn (*see pages 43 and 49*), and to Saturn/Uranus conjunction (*see page 92*). It is possible that these placings could be present in the chart on which you are working.

♒ URANUS IN AQUARIUS

URANUS RULES Aquarius, therefore it is given additional power when it is in this position. Individuals with this placing in their birth chart will have

Uranus Discovered
William Herschel (1738–1822), a British astronomer, discovered the "modern" planet Uranus in 1781.

many of the characteristics of a typical Sun-sign Aquarian. They will be friendly, kind, and humane, and are likely to be very private people who can be difficult to get to know. They will tend to be individualistic in their approach and behaviour, thinking out their own approach to problems rather than relying on advice, however well founded and well meant. They will be easily susceptible to appeals for help, especially from causes with which they feel an emotional affinity, and will be ready not only to subscribe to charities but also to work for them. They will raise money for any fund of which they approve, and will try their utmost to look for ways of easing any suffering that is brought to their attention.

Uranian unpredictability may make them even more individual in character than the average Sun-sign Aquarian, but they may also tend to be somewhat intractable; it will be difficult to woo them from a course of action that may be unsafe. Look at other areas of the birth chart to evaluate how strongly these characteristics are marked. If air signs are prevalent, or emphasized in any way, this placing of Uranus will be even more powerful and influential, and inventiveness and

originality will be joined by a real flair for whatever area of self-expression they may choose.

♓ URANUS IN PISCES

ONE MIGHT EXPECT the combination of the forces of Uranus and Pisces to be a recipe for confusion and disaster: their characteristics are, after all, extremely dissimilar – Pisces being emotional and compassionate, Uranus being very independent and detached. However, those in whose horoscopes Uranus shines from Pisces possess an inspired idealism that is supported by the ability to approach problems with objectivity. A sense of vision combines with kindness and sympathy.

Pisces will always persuade someone to sacrifice self for the good of others, and Uranus is reputed to be the most humane of all the planets. So here is originality, imagination, and inspiration. In combination, these energies will work very well for anyone who has a creative or inventive streak. But for those who are somewhat gullible, the energies can be very susceptible to bad influences: there may be a rather strong tendency to "follow my leader", sometimes in an undesirable direction. Uranus can then bring considerable tension and emotional strain.

If there is a further emphasis on Pisces, or other signs of escapist or self-deceptive tendencies in the chart, the individual may seek to take the easy way out when faced with a crisis, and if a problem is really severe, may even turn to ways of escape such as drugs or alcohol.

Much more likely is that the positive side of the influence will prevail, contributing attractive and interesting characteristics. This is the case even when the planet is not very powerfully placed in the horoscope.

Uranus glyph

PLANETS
SUN
MOON
MERCURY
VENUS
MARS
JUPITER
SATURN
URANUS
NEPTUNE
PLUTO
SIGNS
ARIES
TAURUS
GEMINI
CANCER
LEO
VIRGO
LIBRA
SCORPIO
SAGITTARIUS
CAPRICORN
AQUARIUS
PISCES

NEPTUNE THROUGH THE SIGNS

Neptune, the second of the "modern" planets, takes 165 years to travel round the Sun and through the zodiac, and stays in each of the twelve signs for approximately fourteen years. The planet has a mass influence on the large number of people born during each of its generations, as well as influencing people in their everyday lives. The following interpretations are for the planet in the nine signs that span this century. In 1998 it moves from Capricorn (the sign it entered in the mid-1980s) into Aquarius, where it will remain for thirteen years, travelling slowly towards Pisces.

The Influence of Neptune
Neptune, the Roman god of the sea, can encourage idealism, imagination, and sensitivity, but also carelessness, indecision, and deceit.

NEPTUNE IN GEMINI
1887–89 to 1901–02

THE OVERALL influence of Neptune from Gemini seems to accentuate the sign's communicative nature. During the time when it passed through the sign, the telephone became more widely available. The travel and tourist industries began to burgeon, and the train and car made travel much easier.

People born with Neptune in Gemini have very curious and lively personalities, and are inquisitive but perhaps a little confused by the rapid changes that have occurred during their lifetime. They tend to be wary of new developments in science or changes in the social climate, especially if they have Gemini, Virgo, Sagittarius, or Pisces dominant in their horoscopes.

NEPTUNE IN CANCER
1901–02 to 1915

FOR THE GREAT mass of people born during these years, the emphasis of the planet was on home life. It was a melancholy influence on a whole generation – these people were violently affected by the 1914–18 war when they were children, and then endured the war of 1939–45, when they were parents. In the years between the two world wars life was scarcely less comfortable, with mass unemployment and poverty.

Between 1905 and 1911, Uranus opposed Neptune from Capricorn. This aspect added another negative factor to the lives of this generation. If Neptune is a personal planet in the birth chart, it will increase the inclination to worry, but heighten the subject's sensitivity and intuition, and it also refines and sensitizes any creative work done by the subject.

NEPTUNE IN LEO
1915 to 1928–29

IN LEO, NEPTUNE took on a more positive mood, its influence spiced with the creativity and panache of that sign. The development of the cinema during this period helped alleviate the misery of the First World War and the years of deprivation that followed.

On a personal front, if Neptune is well aspected, or personalized, it will have brought creative potential. It will work particularly well for those people who have Leo or Pisces accentuated in their horoscope, helping them to shape their creative ideas and giving them self-confidence.

NEPTUNE IN VIRGO
1928–29 to 1942–43

THIS WAS THE first generation to move away from accepted religious beliefs. Individuals questioned social conditions and developed idealistic attitudes, prompting a more caring social attitude from that of their contemporaries. Neptune – the ruler of Pisces, a sign closely related to Christianity – was travelling through Pisces' polar sign, Virgo, which by nature is very analytical and critical. Note also that Mercury rules Virgo, and just before Neptune entered the sign, cinema discovered sound and radio grew in popularity.

If Virgo is prominent or Neptune personalized in a birth chart, the imagination will be stimulated and may be expressed through writing. Neptune softens the Virgo character and augments the emotional level, but it can lower self-confidence. The subject's critical faculty undermines the determination to achieve.

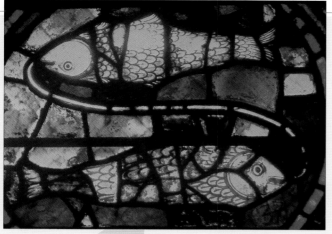

Pisces' Ruler
Pisces, symbolized by two fish swimming in opposite directions, was originally ruled by Jupiter, but Neptune became its ruler after its discovery in 1846.

NEPTUNE IN CAPRICORN
1984–85 to 1998

CAPRICORN IS an earth sign, and the vital issue of the Earth's resources and their conservation is likely to be of the highest priority in the minds of this generation.

Individuals who have Capricorn prominent in their horoscope will find the more strident and severe qualities of Neptune somewhat softened and moderated, while at the same time their rather low emotional level will be increased. They will tend to be cautious but determined, and should be able to control the negative elements of the Neptunian influence, making them less vulnerable to escapism, whether through drugs or self-deception. They are generally very interested in ecology and the problems of the planet. There should be a flair for the creative use of natural materials.

NEPTUNE IN LIBRA
1942–43 to 1956–57

THESE PEOPLE were born either when the Western world was at war, or during the turbulent years of the "Cold War" that followed. Growing up, they became the "flower children" of the late 1960s and early 1970s. Some people from this generation opted out of society; life for them became relaxed, easy, harmonious, and entirely impractical. This was peace-loving Libra married to the self-deceptive, illusory Neptune – surely one of the most striking of all generational influences.

On a personal level, if someone shows escapist or lazy tendencies elsewhere in their chart, these traits will be increased by Neptune in Libra. However, if Libra or Neptune are not prominent in the horoscope, the influence will be weakened.

NEPTUNE IN SCORPIO
1956–57 to 1970–71

THERE COULD scarcely be more of a contrast than between this generation and the previous one. Here are the punks and the hard-rock addicts. Many of these people have had to fight very hard for a decent lifestyle, and Neptune will not help, for when they feel defeated they will easily turn, under the planet's influence, to drugs or other forms of escapism – not the gentle, flower-power drug scene of the 1960s, but intense, self-destructive

escapism. On the other hand, if life goes well, they can be ostentatiously successful. Scorpio rules big business and good living, which many yuppies of this generation enjoyed.

In a personal sense, emotional intensity is increased by Neptune from this sign, and if the planet is well aspected, individuals are likely to express their emotions creatively through some form of art. This heightened sensitivity will be marked only if it is confirmed elsewhere in the chart, or if Scorpio is personalized.

NEPTUNE IN SAGITTARIUS
1970–71 to 1984–85

THE POWERFUL relationship between Neptune and Jupiter (Neptune now rules Pisces, and Pisces was originally ruled by Jupiter) is heightened by Neptune's journey through the Jupiterian sign of Sagittarius. Neptune encourages a strong sense of social justice, and we can expect much that is idealistic, hopeful, and positive from this generation.

Although these young people will have to be tough to cope with the demands of life in the early 21st century, they have a sympathetic side to their personality, and a sense of optimism that should help them solve some of the problems of the future. They will have a strong identification with nature and with animals, and may reject potentially cruel farming methods.

If Sagittarius is prominent in a subject's birth chart, it may indicate one of the leaders of this generation.

NEPTUNE IN AQUARIUS
1998 to c. 2010

ALTHOUGH NEPTUNE had its effect on the lives of those born before the planet was discovered, astrologers have found it difficult to evaluate the influence it can have from signs that it has not occupied within living memory, due to the lack of empirical evidence, practical experience, and observation. The following paragraph is therefore somewhat speculative.

The humanitarian outlook of Aquarius should link well with the gentler characteristics of Neptune, though the detached, independent, and loving traits of Aquarius are light-years away from the sensitive, intuitive emotion of Neptune. Those with the planet well placed in the horoscope should be able to get the best of the two contrasting worlds.

Neptune glyph

PLANETS
SUN
MOON
MERCURY
VENUS
MARS
JUPITER
SATURN
URANUS
NEPTUNE
PLUTO
SIGNS
ARIES
TAURUS
GEMINI
CANCER
LEO
VIRGO
LIBRA
SCORPIO
SAGITTARIUS
CAPRICORN
AQUARIUS
PISCES

PLANETS

SUN

MOON

MERCURY

VENUS

MARS

JUPITER

SATURN

URANUS

NEPTUNE

PLUTO

SIGNS

ARIES

TAURUS

GEMINI

CANCER

LEO

VIRGO

LIBRA

SCORPIO

SAGITTARIUS

CAPRICORN

AQUARIUS

PISCES

PLUTO THROUGH THE SIGNS

Pluto is the most distant and slow-moving of all the planets. It takes around 248 years to complete its journey round the Sun in an elliptical orbit, which results in it spending as brief a time as thirteen years in one sign, and up to thirty-two years in another. Like Neptune and Uranus, it is thought to have a generational influence on individuals, only affecting people strongly if it aspects personal planets in the birth chart. Historically, Pluto is important because it signifies great change and drastic upheaval; change that can either be positive or negative, but always permanent.

PLUTO IN GEMINI
1884 *to* 1912–13

ENORMOUS changes took place during this period; there were important new inventions, and many old ideas – scientific, political, and social – were swept aside by progress. Traditional ideas and values were challenged, and entire concepts seen in a new light. Meanwhile, the evolution of transport began to shrink the world as communications became easier and quicker.

It is not surprising, perhaps, that Pluto from this sign tended to cause mental restlessness. Elderly people with Pluto in Gemini are inquisitive and curious. During their lives they have lived through violent change, and their experience makes them fascinated by the transformations their grandchildren will have to face. They use their experience to inform and enlarge discussion with the younger generations. Their natural Geminian scepticism makes them valuable counsellors.

PLUTO IN CANCER
1912–13 *to* 1937–38

PLUTO ENTERED CANCER just before the First World War, and there began a period during which family life changed greatly – as children were made either temporarily or permanently fatherless. If Pluto is personalized, or Cancer is a

The Influence of Pluto
Pluto, named after the Roman god of the Underworld, is associated with the unconscious, sexuality, and secretiveness. The planet also signifies drastic change.

prominent sign in the birth chart, this placing of Pluto will have a dominant effect on the individual's level of intuition and emotion. If Pluto is negatively aspected by the Sun, Moon, Ascendant, or ruling planet, there can be difficulties in controlling the heightened flow of emotion. If the chart shows good business acumen, Pluto will enhance it further working from Cancer.

PLUTO IN LEO
1937–38 *to* 1957

ONCE AGAIN, at the beginning of Pluto's journey through a new sign, a world war broke out. The evils of nations or individuals aspiring to

world power and domination were highlighted in a most dramatic way, and the strongly domineering elements of Leo were also witnessed. However, some good emerged: the United Nations formed and the protection of the interests of the majority of people was emphasized. Another generational effect of Pluto in Leo has been the speedy development of technology.

The natural power of leadership to be seen in a typical Leo is heightened when Pluto is in that sign, and if the Sun, Moon, or Ascendant are in Leo there can be a power complex. Leo's positive, fiery qualities can be darkened by Pluto, and the personality that can shine so brightly in Leo people may be dimmed. Taureans, Scorpios, and Aquarians born during this period have a tendency towards fanaticism – sometimes benevolently expressed, although it can emerge as obsession. If well directed, the force can be advantageous, motivating the person and those around him or her.

PLUTO IN VIRGO
1957 *to* 1971

BETWEEN LATE 1961 and late 1968, Pluto shared Virgo with Uranus, forming a very potent conjunction that combines the upheaval often instigated by Pluto with Uranus' desire for sudden change. There was a great deal of student unrest, and the values and standards of the older generation were criticized and undermined. Those with a Virgo Sun, Moon, or Ascendant are in a powerful position to make dynamic change. They possess the power to blast the world to fragments or to rid it of much that is unjust.

Pluto can often encourage obsessional tendencies, and if such characteristics are suggested in other areas of the horoscope, this placing of Pluto will increase the possibility. Assess the importance of the Pluto/Uranus conjunction and consider the house placing. If the planets are negatively aspected, the ability to talk freely about problems will be limited, and the subject will tend to worry. If the subject tends to be critical in a particularly harsh way, this may be due to the influence of Pluto: look to other areas of the birth chart to find a rebuttal.

PLUTO IN LIBRA
1971 to 1983–84

SEXUAL PERMISSIVENESS and the relaxation of traditional moral values was a main theme during the period Pluto spent in Libra. The contraceptive pill brought freedom from the fear of pregnancy for many women, and consequently this was an era when the unfettered pursuit of erotic pleasure seemed a desirable and harmless end in itself.

As far as the personal influence goes, Pluto spices up the somewhat placid temperament of Libra, but also increases the Libran tendency to cause problems just for the fun of solving them. This is particularly the case in emotional partnerships, where the pleasure of reconciliation is considered well worth a few hours of unproductive argument. This argumentative trait emerges when Libra is prominent in the horoscope. If Leo is prominent or if Pluto is personalized, then possessiveness and jealousy can be problematic in intimate relationships.

The Philosopher's Art
Descartes discusses astrology with Queen Christina of Sweden, by Pierre-Louis Dumesnil (1698–1781).

PLUTO IN SCORPIO
1983–84 *to* 1995

PLUTO IS AT HOME in this sign and works energetically from here, so one might expect strong symbols of change to emerge from this placing. Lessons are always learned the hard way through Pluto, and this has been a time in which the world has been forced to take stock of the Earth's limited resources of food and fuel. Also during this period, the financial implications of Pluto in its own sign have made themselves felt. The desire to make more money and the increasing expansion of world markets are inspired by this planet.

This is a time when people born with Neptune in Scorpio in their charts (1956 to 1970–71), are making their presence felt as they climb to important positions of power and influence – in politics and financial institutions, as well as less obvious fields such as fashion and music. Pluto's entry into Scorpio has had a powerful effect on the people of this generation, and this is reflected in the preponderance of the Scorpionic colour black in the fashions of the 1980s and the emergence of heavy rock music during this time.

On a personal level, Pluto can bring great intensity and a sense of purpose to individuals from Scorpio, but if the planet receives negative aspects from the Sun, Moon, or ruling planet, it can precipitate psychological problems that must be resolved if the individual is to develop his or her potential. These energies will be stronger and more useful if the Sun, Moon, or Ascendant is also in Scorpio, but they will need to be carefully channelled if they are not to be wasted. If Pluto is conjunct the Midheaven or in the tenth house in a birth chart, this person will most likely have a considerable desire for power.

PLUTO IN SAGITTARIUS
1995 to 2008

PLUTO WAS NOT discovered until 1930, therefore we can only estimate the possibilities of its effect on individuals or on humanity in general. In essence, it is a secretive planet that causes inhibition, making it hard for people to unburden themselves, or talk things through. It can also make them extremely intense, possessive, and jealous. Sagittarius, on the other hand, is open, independent, and freedom-loving – so there are obviously conflicting influences. Pluto can have a purging effect, bringing things out into the open, and it is possible that it may work in this way from Sagittarius, prompting free and frank exchange of views without the onset of revolution. Sagittarius has its serious, philosophical side, so these views will be wise and sage-like, and may contribute beneficently to international conferences and discussions.

Pluto glyph

PLANETS

SUN

MOON

MERCURY

VENUS

MARS

JUPITER

SATURN

URANUS

NEPTUNE

♇
PLUTO

SIGNS

ARIES

TAURUS

GEMINI

CANCER

LEO

VIRGO

LIBRA

SCORPIO

SAGITTARIUS

CAPRICORN

AQUARIUS

PISCES

THE PLANETS THROUGH THE HOUSES

The inner circle of the birth chart is equally divided into twelve houses, running anti-clockwise round the chart from the Ascendant sign. Each house is associated with a different sphere of human life: for example, the first house influences the personality, the fourth house governs home life, and the sixth house affects your health. The first six houses have a personal application, whereas the others relate to more general matters. The position of the planets within the houses at the moment of birth reveal the areas of life that will be most strongly influenced by them.

A depiction of the zodiac from a Nativitat Kalendar *dated 1515.*

PLANETS

☉
SUN

MOON

MERCURY

VENUS

MARS

JUPITER

SATURN

URANUS

NEPTUNE

PLUTO

SIGNS

♈
ARIES

♉
TAURUS

♊
GEMINI

♋
CANCER

♌
LEO

♍
VIRGO

♓
PISCES

THE SUN THROUGH THE HOUSES

The Sun represents our vitality, creativity, and self-expression, and its house position indicates the sphere of life in which these energies will be directed by the individual. For example, the third house is the house of communication, therefore those people with the Sun in the third are articulate, honest, and open, and are well suited to jobs in the media, such as public relations. The Sun rules Leo, therefore it is particularly influential for people who have their Sun or Ascendant placed in Leo. The Sun's influence is at its peak when it is placed in the fifth house, which is the house of Leo and the Sun.

1 THE SUN IN THE FIRST HOUSE

WHEN THE SUN is found in the first house, the subject will have been born very near sunrise, so the Sun and rising sign are likely to be the same, and the subject will be a "double Geminian" or a "double Cancerian". The horoscope will be dominated by the authority of the Sun, and the influence of the planet ruling the Sun and Ascending sign will also be important. Determined and energetic, these people have great personality and qualities of leadership. However, they tend to put themselves first, which can lead to self-absorption and selfishness.

2 THE SUN IN THE SECOND HOUSE

ACQUISITIVE SOULS WITH this placing will treasure their possessions, and gain great pleasure from showing them off. However, they may have to make a conscious effort not to consider their partner as just another possession. Pleasure and comfort are very important to these people (particularly if there are positive aspects between

Classical Bust
The Sun in the second house brings a love of unusual antiques.

the Sun and Jupiter), and they will be prepared to work hard to finance their luxurious life-style.

3 THE SUN IN THE THIRD HOUSE

KNOWLEDGE IS OF great importance to these individuals, and intellectual accomplishments will bring a great sense of fulfilment. The third house is the house of Gemini and Mercury, therefore these people tend to be skilled communicators. Sibling relationships are strongly emphasized by this placing.

4 THE SUN IN THE FOURTH HOUSE

THE ENERGY AND vitality will in this case be focused on creating a secure and happy home and family life. Consequently, the creative energy will centre around the home. This is the house of parenthood, and the Sun sign will dictate this individual's style of parenting. An exuberant, fiery Sun sign will make for an animated, enthusiastic parent, while a more sensitive sign will suggest gentle and intuitive contact with children.

5 THE SUN IN THE FIFTH HOUSE

THE FIFTH HOUSE is the house of Leo and the Sun. It brings energy, creativity, and ambition. Individuals with this placing are proud of their achievements, and not averse to showing them off. This is the house of children, and these people expect their offspring to be as successful as themselves. Love is a particularly important theme, and a passionate and enjoyable sex life is essential. Emotional and physical risks may be taken – indeed, a degree of danger will be positively enjoyed, especially in sporting activities. The gambling urge may be uncomfortably strong.

Brass Lion Doorknocker
The fifth house is traditionally associated with Leo and the Sun.

Pencil Box
Education and schooling are of great importance to those with the Sun in the third house.

PLANETS

☉ SUN

☽ MOON

☿ MERCURY

♀ VENUS

♂ MARS

♃ JUPITER

♄ SATURN

♅ URANUS

♆ NEPTUNE

♇ PLUTO

SIGNS

♈ ARIES

♉ TAURUS

♊ GEMINI

♋ CANCER

♌ LEO

♍ VIRGO

♎ LIBRA

♏

Sewing Basket
Those with the Sun in the sixth are very skilled at intricate manual work.

6 THE SUN IN THE SIXTH HOUSE

HEALTH AND WELLBEING are affected by this house. The Sun sign indicates the areas of the body vulnerable to weakness, but these people should not dwell on their health, for there is a tendency towards hypochondria. However, if the Sun is well aspected (particularly by the Moon or Mars), a positive attitude will prevail. A sense of duty is emphasized by this placing, and these individuals enjoy hard work and being of service to others.

7 THE SUN IN THE SEVENTH HOUSE

A NEED TO relate to others is typical of individuals with this placing – partnership is their ideal. All the vitality of the Sun will be focused on their relationships, and there is a danger that the subjects will allow their partners to dominate them. This is the Venus and Libra house, and the position of Venus in the chart is important. If it shares this house with the Sun, these people may be overly dependent on others.

8 THE SUN IN THE EIGHTH HOUSE

GREAT EMOTIONAL INTENSITY, shrewd intuition, and a yearning for self-knowledge are associated with the Sun in the eighth. There will also be a strong need for sexual satisfaction,

and the creative power of the Sun will make these people ardent and sensuous lovers. Money is also a focal part of the chart for some individuals, and these people are well suited to a financial career.

9 THE SUN IN THE NINTH HOUSE

CHALLENGING JOURNEYS, for both mind and body, are guaranteed to appeal to those born with the Sun in the ninth house. Education, philosophy, and travel are all very important to these individuals, and they will want to broaden their intellectual horizons and develop an individual philosophy of life. The subjects have a rich fantasy life, which can get out of hand, and a practical approach to life must be encouraged.

Leo Cigarette Card
This cigarette card depicts the glyphs and symbols of Leo and the Sun.

10 THE SUN IN THE TENTH HOUSE

AMBITION AND A hunger for fame and recognition are typical of those born with the Sun in the tenth. One way or another, they need to make their mark, and they must feel a strong emotional commitment to the career they take up. Industrious and hardworking, these individuals will channel their formidable energy into their jobs, and will glean great satisfaction from hard work. The Sun sign is of great significance. If the Sun occupies a fire sign, these people will be full of energy and enthusiasm. From an earth sign, the Sun will bring practicality, from air, a lively intelligence, and from water, perception and intuition.

11 THE SUN IN THE ELEVENTH HOUSE

THESE PEOPLE HAVE A strong sense of responsibility to the community, and possess deep-seated humanitarian instincts. They are intensely sociable and friendly, with a wide circle of friends and acquaintances. The ideal career would be charitable fund-raising, which combines their two main interests – charity and socializing. The subjects have an independent streak and, despite their enjoyment of group activities, they can distance themselves from close relationships. To discover whether they may have problems in this area, look at the position of Venus and at the seventh house.

12 THE SUN IN THE TWELFTH HOUSE

PEACE AND QUIET, one's own space, and the time to be alone are all prime concerns for someone with the Sun in the twelfth house. If the Sun sign shares these characteristics, the individual may suffer from a lack of self-confidence. These people need security in order to function well, and feel safest in their own environment. They will be at their happiest working behind the scenes, in a quiet pursuit of excellence but without demanding great acclaim.

Antique Books
People with the Sun in the ninth are ideally suited to careers in publishing and literature.

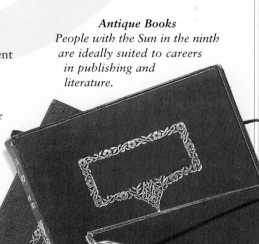

PLANETS

☉ SUN

☽ MOON

☿ MERCURY

♀ VENUS

♂ MARS

♃ JUPITER

♄ SATURN

♅ URANUS

♆ NEPTUNE

♇ PLUTO

SIGNS

♈ ARIES

♉ TAURUS

♊ GEMINI

♋ CANCER

♌ LEO

♍ VIRGO

♎ LIBRA

♐

♑

♒

♓ PISCES

THE MOON THROUGH THE HOUSES

The Moon represents intuition and instinct, and the placement of the Moon indicates the area of life in which the individual will channel his or her emotions. For example, the tenth house governs careers, so people with the Moon in the tenth house will invest all their powerful emotions in their jobs. If Cancer is emphasized by the Sun sign or the Ascendant, the influence of the Moon will be increased. The Moon will also have a strong effect if Taurus is the Sun sign or Ascendant, since the Moon is exalted in Taurus. The more aspects the Moon receives on a chart, the greater the planet's prominence in the horoscope.

1 THE MOON IN THE FIRST HOUSE

THIS PLACING OF the Moon softens the personality and brings a caring, almost maternal aspect to the character. These people are very protective of their loved ones and themselves. They are likely to be intuitive and sensitive, but can also be moody. Emotional responses are heightened and unpredictable. If a sign with a low emotional content is rising, they may be more restrained.

2 THE MOON IN THE SECOND HOUSE

THIS POSITION INDICATES a need for security, and the positive attributes of the Moon (which depend on the sign the planet occupies) will flourish in a stable environment. Emotional happiness may be dependent on a comfortable financial situation.

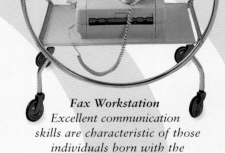

Fax Workstation
Excellent communication skills are characteristic of those individuals born with the Moon in the third house.

If money is short, these individuals are thrown into a state of anxiety, imagining poverty and hardship. A practical influence elsewhere in the horoscope will counter this tendency to worry about money.

3 THE MOON IN THE THIRD HOUSE

COMMUNICATION IS OF the greatest importance to these people and they thrive on constant contact with others. They are eager to learn, but tend only to dip into subjects on a superficial level. Their enthusiasms are rarely long-lasting – they are always yearning to move on to the next item of interest. Open and articulate,

these individuals find it easy to voice their feelings. An empathy with children is typical of this placing.

4 THE MOON IN THE FOURTH HOUSE

SECURITY IN THEIR domestic life is extremely important to these people, and without a stable, happy family background the subjects may function badly in all areas of life. In creating a secure home, the individuals must beware of creating claustrophobic conditions for loved ones. Due to the subjects' love of home life, they may experience emotional upset when their children leave home.

5 THE MOON IN THE FIFTH HOUSE

FROM THIS HOUSE, the Moon's creative drive is directed mainly towards procreation. It is the house of lovemaking, and the subjects tend

Pearl Necklace
Pearls have always been associated with the Moon, because of their spherical shape and luminous gleam.

Cancer Cigarette Card
The glyphs of Cancer and the Moon, the sign and planet of the fourth house, are depicted on this card.

Coin Balance
The Moon in the eighth house is associated with investment and inheritance.

to be ardent, passionate lovers. There is an extroverted streak, which may manifest itself in a desire to show off. The Moon sign can exacerbate or control this tendency – a Piscean Moon, for example, will encourage introversion. The individual may be attracted by risk and danger, but the Sun and Ascending signs may help to counter this unfortunate tendency.

6 THE MOON IN THE SIXTH HOUSE

HEALTH AND WELLBEING are associated with this placing. These individuals may find that their health is governed by their emotions, and any stresses or strains will have an adverse effect. These people may drift into bad habits, such as excessive drinking and smoking, and drug-taking. A regular routine will control such urges. A trine from the Sun to the Moon will encourage steadiness, while squares between the Moon and Neptune may make it difficult to control bad habits.

7 THE MOON IN THE SEVENTH HOUSE

CARING AND DEVOTED, these people tend to seek fulfilment through their romantic relationships. Adoring and easy-going, there is a danger that they may submerge their personality in that of their partner and therefore lose their independence and self-sufficiency. The subjects may provoke arguments with their partners just

because they so enjoy kissing and making up – the Moon sign will dictate the extent of this danger.

8 THE MOON IN THE EIGHTH HOUSE

EMOTION, INSTINCT, and intuition will all be heightened by this placing, especially when Neptune, Pluto, or Scorpio is emphasized elsewhere in the horoscope. Consequently, these individuals are sometimes sensitive to psychic forces. The subjects tend to possess an abundance of sexual energy, which must be positively expressed. Complete trust in loved ones is essential, since any feelings of suspicion and jealousy will mar the love life.

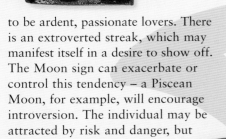

9 THE MOON IN THE NINTH HOUSE

Globe
People with the Moon in the ninth are fond of travel and may live abroad.

THESE PEOPLE have strong spiritual and moral values. In theory eager to study, their fluctuating powers of concentration may obstruct their desire to develop the intellect. A strong Moon sign and good aspects to Mercury and Jupiter are sure to help, however. It is important for these individuals to avoid fantasy and concentrate firmly on fact – the ability to keep both feet firmly on the ground must be encouraged.

10 THE MOON IN THE TENTH HOUSE

THIS PLACING SIGNALS a longing for fame and celebrity. Often the subjects come from a family of high achievers, and will work hard to live up to expectations. These individuals make natural leaders with an ability to inspire

love and respect in large groups of people. They are understanding and sympathetic, with a longing to put the world to rights. An ideal position for those interested in politics.

11 THE MOON IN THE ELEVENTH HOUSE

THIS INDIVIDUAL WILL always want to be a member of a group or club – perhaps he or she felt unaccepted by peers as a child. There may be a tendency to rely too much on friends and lovers, along with an inability to stand alone and make independent judgements. This is the Aquarian house, and due to the influence of Aquarius, these people can be so private that others find it almost impossible to get close to them. Alternatively, their need to be loved may be so strong that it alienates friends and partners.

12 THE MOON IN THE TWELFTH HOUSE

FULL OF NATURAL kindness and emotional sensitivity, these people possess a real concern for other people, and are prepared to make sacrifices to keep others happy. Beneath their extrovert exteriors, these individuals tend to be rather shy and sensitive. From time to time, they have a deep need for solitude, which enables them to engage in psychological and spiritual renewal. However, they must not allow themselves to become emotionally isolated.

Acoustic Guitar
Artistic creativity is characteristic of the twelfth house. People with this placing are often talented musicians or artists.

PLANETS

SUN

MOON

MERCURY

VENUS

MARS

JUPITER

SATURN

URANUS

NEPTUNE

PLUTO

SIGNS

ARIES

TAURUS

GEMINI

CANCER

LEO

VIRGO

LIBRA

MERCURY THROUGH THE HOUSES

The sphere of life governed by the house that Mercury occupies will be given much thought by the individual. The way in which the mind works – whether he or she thinks logically or intuitively, is a natural worrier or completely carefree, is blindly optimistic or totally pessimistic – will, of course, depend on the sign Mercury occupies and, to a certain extent, the aspects it receives. However, when interpreting the influence of Mercury's house position, it is always important to consider whether the subject likes to plan constructively and sensibly, or prefers to be carried away by exciting new ideas.

1 MERCURY IN THE FIRST HOUSE

THESE PEOPLE ARE talkative and versatile, but must learn to avoid superficiality and hypochondria. The aspects Mercury receives must be considered, for they will colour the attitude to life. Mercury's sign placing is also important. If there are negative aspects from the Moon, Mars, or Uranus, nervous tension could cause stomach upsets or migraines. The nearer Mercury is to the Ascendant, the more powerful its influence – to the point where it can affect the whole birth chart.

2 MERCURY IN THE SECOND HOUSE

The attitude to money will be astute, but there is a tendency to get involved in dubious get-rich-quick schemes. The aspects received by Mercury, and the sign placing of the planet, will reveal just how damaging this tendency may be.

Gemini Cigarette Card
This card shows the glyphs of Gemini and Mercury, the sign and planet of the third house.

Mobile Phone
The urge to communicate is very strong when Mercury occupies the third house.

Positive aspects from Saturn will have a steadying effect, but negative aspects from Neptune could signal potential confusion, deceit, and fraud. This is the house of Venus and Taurus, and because Mercury rules the hands, these people make skilled masseurs, both professionally and when making love.

3 MERCURY IN THE THIRD HOUSE

MERCURY'S INFLUENCE is particularly powerful in this position, because the third house is connected with Mercury and Gemini. These people are inquisitive and gregarious, with a need to communicate, but may be more interested in how they express themselves than in what they say. Keeping up to date with the latest developments is important to these alert and perceptive individuals, and they tend to be voracious readers of newspapers and magazines.

4 MERCURY IN THE FOURTH HOUSE

HOME AND FAMILY will be of special importance, and these people will relate to their partners and children in the manner of the sign in which Mercury finds itself. They tend to move house frequently, and this tendency will be more marked if the Sun and Moon are in negative aspect to each other, indicating an inner discontent that finds expression in restlessness. This is the Cancer/Moon house, and the subject's mother may have had a particularly stimulating influence.

Royal Flush
Mercury in the fifth brings a gambling instinct. Whether it is logical or intuitive depends on the sign that Mercury occupies.

PLANETS

SUN

MOON

MERCURY

VENUS

MARS

JUPITER

SATURN

URANUS

NEPTUNE

PLUTO

SIGNS

ARIES

TAURUS

GEMINI

CANCER

LEO

VIRGO

LIBRA

SCORPIO

SAGITTARIUS

CAPRICORN

AQUARIUS

PISCES

5 MERCURY IN THE FIFTH HOUSE

THIS HOUSE is important where love affairs are concerned, but there is more than a hint of duality in this placing, largely because Mercury is basically changeable. These people will be attracted by leisure pursuits that challenge the intellect – chess, for instance – provided that Mercury is in a sign that bestows patience.

6 MERCURY IN THE SIXTH HOUSE

WORKING FROM THE Virgo house, Mercury's influence is strong. Diet is of great interest to these people, and they will enjoy vegetarian and health foods, homeopathic remedies, and holistic medicine. If there are any signs in the horoscope that suggest anxiety, they will not be alleviated by this placing of Mercury. The best solution to this anxiety is invariably to try to adopt a practical approach. Routine tends to be of great importance to these people.

Gavel and Block
Mercury in the seventh house emphasizes negotiation. Lawyers are likely to have this placing.

Book Collection
There is a strong hunger for knowledge and intellectual development when Mercury is in the ninth house.

7 MERCURY IN THE SEVENTH HOUSE

FRIENDSHIP WITHIN relationships is important here. Gullibility can be a problem, particularly if Mercury is in Libra or Pisces. The subjects make excellent salespeople and business partners. If the law is indicated in other areas of the chart (such as a powerful Jupiter, or a Sagittarian Sun or Midheaven), this placing may indicate a talented lawyer.

8 MERCURY IN THE EIGHTH HOUSE

THIS HOUSE CAN have a psychic influence. If the Moon and Mercury are adversely aspected to each other or to the Sun, the individual may find it too difficult to cope with the occult. If there are no adverse indications, and earth signs are prominent, these people may make excellent mediums – though proper instruction should always be sought before dabbling in any form of the occult. The solving of mysteries, in the widest sense, may be possible. This placing of Mercury also suggests a powerful preoccupation with sex, and a strong fantasy life.

9 MERCURY IN THE NINTH HOUSE

MERCURY IS VERY sympathetically placed in the ninth house, the house concerned with the intellect, but there is likely to be a very strong desire to escape, resulting in a fascination with travel. These people are suited to work in libraries, book shops, art galleries, and universities, and those with a Sagittarian Sun sign or Ascendant will be eternal students.

10 MERCURY IN THE TENTH HOUSE

THESE PEOPLE LIKE to frequently change their jobs, and even their careers. Ideally, their work needs to have a good mix of intellectual stimulation, responsibility, and mobility. This is the house of the father, and subjects may think and plan in a manner reminiscent of their father. On a deeper level, the voice of the "father" may be the inner voice of conscience.

11 MERCURY IN THE ELEVENTH HOUSE

SOCIAL INTERCOURSE WILL be of the greatest importance – these people simply must communicate, and will possess a very large circle of friends and acquaintances. Every spare moment is likely to be occupied by getting out and about. The subjects may find fulfilment in charity work, where their communicative skills will be useful. The Sun and Mercury live closely together, and Mercury in the eleventh house and the Sun in the twelfth may sometimes suggest a spell of peace and quiet, and the subject must remember to take this hint.

12 MERCURY IN THE TWELFTH HOUSE

MERCURY IS LOGICAL, while the twelfth house is intuitive and emotional. This essential conflict can be dealt with by rationalizing the intuition and channelling the emotions, but there is likely to be another conflict in the need both for social intercourse and for solitude. These people often possess a love of literature, particularly poetry. If they have a religious bent, their faith is absolute, but whatever their beliefs, they always promote the power of positive thinking.

Radio Microphone
Mercury in the twelfth often brings a love of working in the media, especially in radio.

PLANETS

☉ SUN

☽ MOON

☿ MERCURY

♀ VENUS

♂ MARS

♃ JUPITER

♄ SATURN

♅ URANUS

♆ NEPTUNE

♇ PLUTO

SIGNS

♈ ARIES

♉ TAURUS

♊ GEMINI

♋ CANCER

♌ LEO

♍ VIRGO

♎ LIBRA

♏

♐

♑

♒

♓ PISCES

VENUS THROUGH THE HOUSES

Each house governs a different sphere of human life, just as each planet affects a different aspect of the personality. Venus through the houses provides a valuable insight into the social, romantic, and artistic aspects of the character. Friendships and romantic alliances will be formed within the sphere of life ruled by the house that Venus occupies. For example, the ninth house covers long journeys; therefore those with Venus in the ninth house are likely to meet their loved one while travelling. The influence of the planet is greatly increased when it occupies the second and seventh houses – the Taurean and Libran houses respectively.

1 VENUS IN THE FIRST HOUSE

THESE CHARMING, ATTRACTIVE people need to love and be loved, and a stable emotional relationship is essential to their happiness. Good company and conversation are very important to them, as is a leisurely, convivial atmosphere. They appear laid back, but this relaxed attitude may be feigned. Although considerate and kind, these people can be just a little resentful. Their metabolism may be sluggish, and regular exercise is essential to keep them in good shape. The closer Venus is to the Ascendant, the more powerful the planet's effect.

Cigarette Card
This shows the glyphs of Taurus and Venus, the planet and sign associated with the second house.

2 VENUS IN THE SECOND HOUSE

VENUS WORKS POWERFULLY from this, the Taurus/Venus house. Material possessions are important to these acquisitive individuals, and they love collecting beautiful objects. An element of possessiveness may be present in the personality, and the

Antique Coffee-pot
Acquiring beautiful possessions is important to people with Venus in the second house.

subject could regard a partner as just another possession. These people like to look good and win the admiration of others. They are extremely generous, but this may be in an attempt to buy love and attention, particularly if Venus is in a showy sign such as Leo.

3 VENUS IN THE THIRD HOUSE

CLOSE AND HARMONIOUS family relationships are very important to these sympathetic and understanding individuals. The perfect students, they relish an intellectual challenge and demand constant mental stimulation. A glossy encyclopedia will make the perfect gift. These individuals are friendly and outgoing, and are guaranteed to be at the centre of a large social circle. They are at their happiest entertaining their many friends in a lively and animated atmosphere.

4 VENUS IN THE FOURTH HOUSE

FOR THOSE BORN with Venus in the fourth house, the mother-child relationship is significant. These individuals tend to identify with and emulate their mothers. As a result, there may be problems when they leave home for the first time. These people will work hard to create a home that is a haven of calm and comfort. The subjects are loving and supportive parents, but may spoil their children.

5 VENUS IN THE FIFTH HOUSE

THIS PLACING OF Venus emphasizes creative ability and a love of the arts. These people are true romantics, but have a tendency to place their lovers on a pedestal, which can lead to heartache and disillusionment. They love luxury and often display an innate elegance and sense of style. A fascination with financial risk can have disastrous consequences, so a gambling instinct must be kept on a tight rein.

Flowers
People with Venus in the fourth house love fresh flowers.

Piggy Bank
Venus in the eighth house is traditionally associated with fortunate inheritance.

6 VENUS IN THE SIXTH HOUSE

FOND OF GOOD FOOD and wine, these people are not always equally fond of exercise. The metabolism may be slow, resulting in a tendency to put on weight, (possibly exacerbated by thyroid problems), and regular exercise should be encouraged. A steady work routine is essential, and may help to boost the metabolism. They appreciate good manners, and will not tolerate uncouth behaviour in others.

7 VENUS IN THE SEVENTH HOUSE

THOSE WITH VENUS in the seventh house may rush into love affairs too hastily, due to their yearning for a secure long term relationship. There is a danger that these people will identify with their partner so much that their own personality is suppressed. Such tendencies must be discouraged. They will thrive and prosper when settled in a well-rounded alliance that combines close friendship with physical passion. If Venus is inhibited by the Moon, Saturn, or Uranus, the subject may give up too easily if problems develop in his or her relationship.

8 VENUS IN THE EIGHTH HOUSE

FROM THIS HOUSE, the intensity of the individual's emotions and passions is increased, and consequently these people may be jealous and demanding. However, they are also kind and considerate, especially if Venus occupies a water sign. An imaginative and rewarding sex life is likely, unless Venus is inhibited by Saturn or Pluto. There may be profit from an inheritance, and in addition there is usually a well-developed business sense and flair for investment.

9 VENUS IN THE NINTH HOUSE

TRAVEL IS OF great importance to individuals born with Venus in the ninth house. These people often marry foreigners and move away from the country of their birth. A philosophical attitude to life may be apparent, along with an innate desire to make the world a better place to live in. If the subject is motivated and energetic (depending on the position of Mars), great efforts will be made to achieve this ambition, and they may work for a charity or in the peace movement.

Antique Compass
People with Venus in the ninth house will enjoy holiday romances in exotic destinations.

10 VENUS IN THE TENTH HOUSE

THE SUBJECTS ARE happiest working as part of a team, and are good at establishing a friendly, congenial rapport with their colleagues. They may not be suited to freelance work, as they find it hard to be disciplined when working alone. A good salary is important, but is not a primary consideration – job fulfilment is more important to these individuals than financial success. These people identify wholeheartedly with the ambitions of their partners and encourage them in their aspirations.

11 VENUS IN THE ELEVENTH HOUSE

A LIVELY AND action-packed social life is important to people born with Venus in the eleventh house, and they usually possess an abundance of friends and acquaintances. These individuals have a flair for organizing social events and are talented at fundraising, for their social skills are combined with charitable and tender hearts. They work well with others, and are ideal committee members. Charming and friendly, these people work hard to win admiration and praise from others, for they have an innate desire to please.

12 VENUS IN THE TWELFTH HOUSE

WHEN IN LOVE, these hopeless romantics tend to be extremely secretive. They will strive to conceal their deepest emotions from their friends, and may even find it difficult to articulate their feelings to their potential lovers. These individuals can suffer from a strong sense of isolation, which may result in comfort eating and drinking. Alternatively, solace may be sought in religion. The influence of Venus is particularly strong if the planet is conjunct with the Ascendant.

Heart Key-ring
Venus in the twelfth indicates a starry-eyed romantic.

PLANETS

SUN

MOON

MERCURY

VENUS

MARS

JUPITER

SATURN

URANUS

NEPTUNE

PLUTO

SIGNS

ARIES

TAURUS

GEMINI

CANCER

LEO

VIRGO

LIBRA

SCORPIO

SAGITTARIUS

CAPRICORN

AQUARIUS

PISCES

MARS THROUGH THE HOUSES

The dynamic, fiery planet Mars energizes and invigorates the affairs of the house it occupies in the birth chart. The individual will expend considerable energy on the sphere of life denoted by their house, in the manner suggested by the sign in which Mars falls. The energy and power of Mars may be expressed positively or negatively, depending on the sign the planet occupies. For example, a person with Mars in Aries in the second house, the house governing the acquisition of money, will channel their abundance of brash Arien energy into attaining financial success – perhaps treading on a few toes in the process.

1 MARS IN THE FIRST HOUSE

THE FIRST HOUSE is ruled by Aries, and when Mars occupies this house the planet dominates the entire horoscope. The potency of Mars enlivens the characteristics of the ascending sign, and these people have a tremendous will to succeed. Hasty and hotheaded, they can be impatient and do not suffer fools gladly. The subjects enjoy exercise, and possess both physical and mental daring. Carelessness can lead to accidents, but their recuperative powers are excellent.

2 MARS IN THE SECOND HOUSE

THE ACQUISITION OF wealth and possessions is emphasized here. The sign that Mars occupies indicates how money will be acquired: through careful investment, skilful dealings, or a long hard slog. These people are passionate and can be possessive. If Mars occupies Taurus, Cancer, or Scorpio, the subject may possess a fiery temper and will not be quick to forget an insult.

Cigarette Card
This cigarette card depicts the symbols of Aries, the sign associated with the first house.

3 MARS IN THE THIRD HOUSE

INDIVIDUALS WITH MARS in the third house have a contentious turn of mind, and enjoy lively debate. They are naturally inquisitive, and eager to find a solution to every problem. Dynamic and energetic, these people thrive on excitement, but should not become too reckless. They will fight hard for their beliefs, and their energy and commitment will prove inspirational to others.

4 MARS IN THE FOURTH HOUSE

THE FOURTH HOUSE governs family and home life, in particular the relationship between mother and child. This placing indicates a strong and forceful mother, who plays a dominant role in her child's life. The subjects tend to be restless and may move house frequently. They are often skilled at DIY, and their powerful Martian energy will be directed towards improving and redecorating the home.

5 MARS IN THE FIFTH HOUSE

MARS IN THE fifth house underlines sexual pleasure and an active and happy love life. These people make passionate lovers, and demand an equally enthusiastic response from their partners. Bold and adventurous, they enjoy flirting with danger and often possess a strong gambling instinct. The sign in which Mars is placed will indicate whether this reckless streak is likely to get out of hand – the cautious influence of Capricorn or Virgo, for example, should prevent excessive risk-taking.

Crossed Swords
People with Mars in the third house will cross swords with anyone who dares to disagree with them.

6 MARS IN THE SIXTH HOUSE

HERE ARE THE world's workers. Although both conscientious and industrious, they have surprisingly

Roulette Wheel
Those with Mars in the fifth will wager everything on the spin of the wheel.

PLANETS
SUN
MOON
MERCURY
VENUS
MARS
JUPITER
SATURN
URANUS
NEPTUNE
PLUTO
SIGNS
ARIES
TAURUS
GEMINI
CANCER
LEO

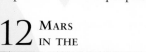

Magnifying Glass
Mars in the eighth brings a fascination with investigation and research.

little patience with dull routine. If there is no indication of nervous tension elsewhere in the horoscope, and Mars is free from negative aspects from the Moon, Mercury, or Uranus, this placing will stimulate the nervous system, and the subject is likely to possess an incisive and discriminating mind. Physically, stress will affect their health, and these people may find that they are susceptible to skin complaints when under strain.

7 MARS IN THE SEVENTH HOUSE

MARS FROM THE seventh house emphasizes partnerships, and these people will channel the powerful energy of Mars into creating a successful relationship. Provided that the harsher, quarrelsome side of the Martian influence is contained, this placing is invaluable for couples who decide to work together. It encourages their joint objectives, and prompts them to make their relationship a positive expression of purpose and direction. From this house, Mars will bring a degree of energy and passion that will ensure a rewarding and fulfilling sex life.

8 MARS IN THE EIGHTH HOUSE

BEFORE THE DISCOVERY of Pluto, Mars ruled Scorpio, and its position in the Scorpio house is still very influential. These people have a powerful sex drive, coupled with emotional intensity. Their intuition is also sharpened by this placing, and it will be especially well-tuned when it comes to selecting a lover. A secretive streak and a fascination with investigation may lead to a career in police work or private

detection. These people often have a shrewd interest in finance, and the sign Mars inhabits will indicate how successful the subject will be in this sphere of life.

9 MARS IN THE NINTH HOUSE

IMBUED WITH AN adventurous, wayfaring spirit, these people love travel and are not stay-at-home types. They also want to broaden their intellectual horizons, and further education will appeal, particularly if there are positive aspects from the Sun or Moon to Saturn. Hard-working and energetic, they can become restless and impatient if their progress is obstructed. Relaxation techniques may bring a calmer outlook on life.

10 MARS IN THE TENTH HOUSE

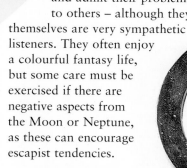

Botanist's Specimen Bag
An interest in ecology and the natural world is often displayed by people with Mars in the eleventh house.

THESE PEOPLE ARE driven by a powerful desire to get to the top. Mars will bring them ambition and a longing for fame and status, especially if the planet is conjunct with the Midheaven. If Mars receives negative aspects from the personal planets or from Uranus, the subject may be impatient and find tension hard to deal with. Consequently, when faced with cautious and more plodding colleagues, tempestuous quarrels may result. The tenth house has a connection with the father, and the individual's early life may have been strongly affected by an over-assertive paternal presence.

11 MARS IN THE ELEVENTH HOUSE

FRIENDSHIP IS VERY important to these outgoing extroverts, and all the energy of Mars will be directed towards forming relationships. These individuals are lively and dynamic, bringing a sense of fun and excitement to every occasion. However, the more aggressive and argumentative side of Mars may bring a quarrelsome side to the personality. Faced with any display of suffering, they will be positive and combative, responding with action rather than sympathy. In affairs of the heart, Mars encourages detachment – independence is very important to these people.

12 MARS IN THE TWELFTH HOUSE

THESE COMPASSIONATE PEOPLE identify strongly with human suffering and will channel all their Martian energy into alleviating the hardships of others. They are well suited to a career in the caring professions, such as social work. These individuals tend to be rather secretive, and may find it hard to open up and admit their problems to others – although they themselves are very sympathetic listeners. They often enjoy a colourful fantasy life, but some care must be exercised if there are negative aspects from the Moon or Neptune, as these can encourage escapist tendencies.

Handcuffs
The twelfth house is traditionally associated with imprisonment.

PLANETS

SUN

MOON

MERCURY

VENUS

MARS

JUPITER

SATURN

URANUS

NEPTUNE

PLUTO

SIGNS

ARIES

TAURUS

GEMINI

CANCER

VIRGO

LIBRA

SCORPIO

PISCES

PLANETS

SUN

MOON

MERCURY

VENUS

MARS

JUPITER

SATURN

URANUS

NEPTUNE

PLUTO

SIGNS

ARIES

TAURUS

GEMINI

CANCER

LEO

VIRGO

LIBRA

SCORPIO

SAGITTARIUS

CAPRICORN

AQUARIUS

PISCES

JUPITER THROUGH THE HOUSES

Jupiter encourages both mental and physical expansion, and the planet's potential for personal growth and development will manifest itself in the different spheres of life covered by each house placing. Jupiter will bring ease and facility to those areas ruled by the house in which Jupiter is placed. For example, those people with Jupiter in the ninth, the house of thought and philosophy, will embrace new ideas with enthusiasm and an open mind. Generally, Jupiter brings a positive outlook on life unless the planet is negatively aspected. If afflicted, Jupiter may encourage exaggeration and self-aggrandizement.

1 JUPITER IN THE FIRST HOUSE

PEOPLE WITH JUPITER in the first house will live their lives to the full, brimming over with optimistic enthusiasm. They possess an enviable breadth of vision, and even if a meticulous sign, such as Virgo, is rising, the individual can concentrate on the broad outline of a situation, rather than focusing on details. Although open and honest, these people may be a little boisterous and have a tendency to exaggerate if Jupiter is afflicted by the Sun, Moon, or Mars. If this more excitable side of Jupiter is dominant, they must be encouraged to cultivate a more philosophical outlook on life.

2 JUPITER IN THE SECOND HOUSE

THIS HOUSE EMPHASIZES the materialistic side of Jupiter, and money and possessions are of particular importance. These people are shrewd financiers, and should enjoy good fortune. However, if Jupiter is afflicted, especially by

Table Setting
People with Jupiter in the first house enjoy fine food but will have to watch their weight.

a square or opposition from Venus, money may go out as fast as it comes in, resulting in bad investment and debt. When it comes to relationships, the subjects are generous to a fault, showering their partners with gifts. However, they must be careful not to try to purchase love and affection.

3 JUPITER IN THE THIRD HOUSE

JUPITER IS THE planet of the intellect, and the third (Geminian) house has strong connections with the mind. As a result, these individuals thrive on intellectual challenges and enjoy constant mental activity. They like to keep abreast of current thought, and are incisive social commentators. These people have excellent communication skills, and thrive on stimulating discussion and debate. Travel is important, unless Jupiter is in a fixed sign.

4 JUPITER IN THE FOURTH HOUSE

A HARMONIOUS FAMILY life is essential for these individuals. They have close relationships with their parents and siblings, and, in turn, will be wise, loving, and supportive parents. The home is seen as a retreat from the stresses of daily life. If these people want to invest, property is the answer – home ownership will bring them the security they need.

5 JUPITER IN THE FIFTH HOUSE

JUPITER OFFERS OPTIMISM and enthusiasm from the fifth house. Charming and sociable, these people often possess a large circle of friends. However, they must keep their liveliness in check, lest they become too exhibitionistic. If Jupiter is squared or opposed by the Sun, the Moon, or Mars, there may be severe

Antique Flask
Jupiter in the second house indicates a love of beautiful and expensive objects.

Personal Organizer
Jupiter in the sixth house brings enviable organizational skills.

Sagittarius Cigarette Card
This card depicts the glyph and symbols of Sagittarius, the planet ruled by Jupiter.

financial losses due to gambling. A well-aspected Saturn will provide a stabilizing influence. The subjects are good with children, and make inspiring teachers and positive, supportive parents.

6 JUPITER IN THE SIXTH HOUSE

JUPITER IN THE sixth house concerns itself with physical health. A slow metabolism may be combined with a love of good food, and the subjects put on weight easily. Discipline is needed, and a steady exercise regime will benefit the subject. These people love helping others, and show great generosity with both their time and money. They are conscientious and committed workers.

7 JUPITER IN THE SEVENTH HOUSE

RELATIONSHIPS ARE all-important to these people. Consequently, they will throw themselves enthusiastically into the quest for a partner and may settle down at too young an age. Intellectual rapport with a lover will provide a strong and enduring basis for a happy relationship. The subjects make excellent business partners. They tend to enjoy good fortune

in their business dealings, largely because they are full of innovative ideas that soon lead to expansion.

8 JUPITER IN THE EIGHTH HOUSE

A STIMULATING AND exciting sex life is essential for these individuals. If their partner is not passionate and responsive, they may look elsewhere for sexual satisfaction. Financial gain through investment is strongly indicated by this placing of Jupiter, and if the planet is well aspected the subject will have a good head for business. If Jupiter occupies an earth sign in particular, extremely profitable investments are likely.

9 JUPITER IN THE NINTH HOUSE

THE PURSUIT OF knowledge is the focal point of the ninth house. These people possess great intellectual ability, a love of study, and breadth of vision. A passion for travel is often combined with a flair for languages, and the subjects may live and work abroad. However, if Jupiter occupies a fire or air sign, or is negatively aspected by Mercury or Mars, love of travel may manifest itself as extreme restlessness.

10 JUPITER IN THE TENTH HOUSE

AMBITIOUS, DRIVEN success-seekers, individuals born with Jupiter in the tenth house are determined to excel at everything they turn their hand to. They are likely to achieve very high standing in the community through sheer hard work. However, they must make sure that their labours do not cause them to neglect family life.

Artist's Palette
The solitary pursuits of painting and writing will appeal to those with Jupiter in the twelfth house.

Diplomat's Leather Case
Tact and diplomacy are characteristic of those born with Jupiter in the eleventh house.

11 JUPITER IN THE ELEVENTH HOUSE

THESE INDIVIDUALS ARE sociable and warm-hearted. They care deeply for their friends, and will want to do their bit to help humanity at large. The subjects generate a great deal of energy and enthusiasm, and make excellent campaigners and fund-raisers. They work particularly well as part of a team, and do not enjoy solitary endeavour.

12 JUPITER IN THE TWELFTH HOUSE

SPIRITUAL AND SELFLESS, these people may possess deep-seated religious or spiritual beliefs. These individuals tend to work best when alone. However, they must not be allowed to become too introspective and solitary. The subjects are kind and compassionate, with a strong sense of social responsibility. As a result, they are ideally suited to a career in the caring or medical professions.

URANUS
NEPTUNE
PLUTO
SIGNS
ARIES
TAURUS
GEMINI
CANCER
LEO
VIRGO
LIBRA
SCORPIO
SAGITTARIUS
CAPRICORN
AQUARIUS
PISCES

PLANETS

SUN

MOON

MERCURY

VENUS

MARS

JUPITER

♄
SATURN

URANUS

NEPTUNE

PLUTO

SIGNS

♈
ARIES

♉
TAURUS

♊
GEMINI

♋
CANCER

♌
LEO

♍
VIRGO

♎
LIBRA

♏

SATURN THROUGH THE HOUSES

Restrictive Saturn provides a necessary counterbalance to expansive Jupiter. Saturn imposes essential limits and encourages self-discipline. It regulates and controls personal growth and development. The house that Saturn occupies reveals the areas in which the individual may experience particular difficulties and hardships during his or her passage though life. Progress in these areas may only be made after a great deal of effort. The aspects that Saturn receives from other planets will provide an indication of whether it will be a negative or a positive influence on other areas of the subject's life.

1 SATURN IN THE FIRST HOUSE

SATURN, FROM THIS house, can bring inhibition and shyness, and the closer Saturn is to the Ascendant, the stronger the effect will be. However, common sense and self-confidence will develop as the individual matures. Carefully study the effects of the sign in which Saturn is placed: its characteristics will be influential. This placing tends to lower physical vitality, which may be exacerbated by a touch of hypochondria.

2 SATURN IN THE SECOND HOUSE

PEOPLE WITH SATURN in the second house will have to work hard for every penny they earn. However, this does not mean that financial

Legal Documents
Lawyers and accountants often have Saturn in the second house.

Wool and Knitting Needles
People with Saturn in the fifth house work well with natural materials such as wool or wood.

success is unlikely, and when it comes there will be a considerable sense of pride and satisfaction. Saturn may inhibit overt displays of emotion, but these individuals will eventually become confident and learn to relax enough to express sensual pleasure in a sexual relationship.

3 SATURN IN THE THIRD HOUSE

THESE INDIVIDUALS TEND to be sensible and practical, particularly good at laying sound, long-term plans. Due to the influence of Saturn, they excel when it comes to concentrated mental effort. From this house, Saturn often shows its effect early in the life of the subjects, who may dislike school and be very miserable there, yet will still manage to succeed against all the odds. This is a prime example of Saturn working in its usual dour way, granting success only after hardship. These people may blame their lack of success on poor education or unjust employers.

4 SATURN IN THE FOURTH HOUSE

SATURN IN THE fourth house indicates a strict and oppressive upbringing. These people may have had remote and undemonstrative parents, who withheld affection and approval. As a result, these individuals can be introspective and inhibited when it comes to showing their feelings. The subjects must work hard to break this pattern and to form a closer bond with their own children.

5 SATURN IN THE FIFTH HOUSE

THIS PLACING indicates a dogmatic, overbearing father figure. As a result, these people may feel inadequate and unable to express their emotions for fear of rejection. Only if they can overcome their inhibitions will they find happiness and contentment. They are extremely ambitious for their children, and must not be too pushy. When it comes to affairs of the heart, these individuals are extremely serious. They can be rather lacking in humour and must work hard to develop a sense of fun.

Dental Tools
People with Saturn in the sixth house often have weak or sensitive teeth.

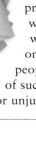

Collectors' Cards
Saturn in the eighth house
indicates someone who is suited
to a career in engineering.

6 SATURN IN THE SIXTH HOUSE

HARD WORK IS second nature to those with Saturn in the sixth house. However, these people must beware of becoming bogged down in routine. They may feel that they have not taken the right career path, and often complain about their jobs. However, because the subjects tend to lack in self-confidence, they find it hard to change direction. They must overcome their lack of self-esteem and develop more self-assurance.

7 SATURN IN THE SEVENTH HOUSE

THIS IS THE house of partnership, and a responsible and mature attitude to relationships is typical of these people. When it comes to long-term commitment, the subjects can be swayed by mercenary considerations, choosing a partner for their wealth and status rather than on the basis of mutual attraction. These people are generally loving and loyal in their romantic relationships, but if Saturn is badly aspected, there may be poor communication between partners.

8 SATURN IN THE EIGHTH HOUSE

THOSE BORN WITH Saturn in the eighth are disciplined thinkers, with outstanding powers of concentration. This placing also indicates an involvement in financial affairs, and these people are well suited to careers in banking or insurance. If Saturn is afflicted, there may be litigation regarding money or inheritances. Relationships may be marred by mistrust and jealousy, but in time the subjects will learn from their mistakes and should develop a more relaxed attitude to their partners.

9 SATURN IN THE NINTH HOUSE

Capricorn Cigarette Card
This card shows the glyphs
and symbols of Capricorn,
the sign ruled by Saturn.

SERIOUS-MINDED AND cerebral, these people have a strong interest in religion, philosophy, and higher education. They will constantly strive to extend their knowledge, and have the ability to become totally absorbed in their work. Many teachers and professors have this placing. Due to the restrictive nature of Saturn, the subjects may fear and dislike travel, especially flying. If negatively aspected, Saturn may bring shyness and a lack of self-confidence.

10 SATURN IN THE TENTH HOUSE

THIS POSITION is a very strong one since the tenth house corresponds to Capricorn, the sign ruled by Saturn. These individuals are motivated and ambitious. Material success is their aim, and if Saturn is well aspected, their hard work, honesty, and high moral standards will guarantee them great success and acclaim. However, if the planet is badly aspected, the reverse is true. These individuals can appear reserved, and even unfriendly, but this is only due to their innate fear of failure and rejection.

11 SATURN IN THE ELEVENTH HOUSE

ALTHOUGH THEIR SOCIAL life is very important to them, these people have only a small and select band of friends. Those closest to them tend to be older and wiser, with a mature and settled outlook on life. These individuals are dutiful and serious, and feel guilty when they spend time on frivolous but enjoyable pastimes. They enjoy solitary pursuits, and devote much time and energy to their wide range of hobbies.

12 SATURN IN THE TWELFTH HOUSE

THESE PEOPLE ENJOY their own company and need to withdraw from the world every now and then to recharge their energy supplies. Quiet and self-involving hobbies appeal, such as reading, listening to music, and home crafts. They are happy to work behind the scenes, and do not seek acclaim or glory.

Dressmakers' Patterns
Saturn in the twelfth house
brings a love of quiet, tranquil
hobbies such as sewing,
reading, and cookery.

PLANETS

SUN

MOON

MERCURY

VENUS

MARS

JUPITER

SATURN

URANUS

NEPTUNE

PLUTO

SIGNS

ARIES

TAURUS

GEMINI

CANCER

LEO

VIRGO

PLANETS

SUN

MOON

MERCURY

VENUS

MARS

JUPITER

SATURN

♅
URANUS

NEPTUNE

PLUTO

SIGNS

♈
ARIES

♉
TAURUS

♊
GEMINI

♋
CANCER

♌

♎
LIBRA

♏
SCORPIO

♐
SAGITTARIUS

♑
CAPRICORN

♒

URANUS THROUGH THE HOUSES

The planet Uranus is primarily associated with change and development. The position that Uranus occupies in the houses reveals the area of life in which unexpected developments and sudden changes may occur. For example, the third house governs the mind and education, therefore individuals with this placing may make rather unpredictable pupils, alternating between the very top and the very bottom of the class. Uranus rules Aquarius, so this planet is of particular importance for anyone with the Sun or Ascendant in Aquarius. The planet's effect is at its strongest when it occupies the eleventh (Aquarian) house.

1 URANUS IN THE FIRST HOUSE

THESE PEOPLE HAVE a longing for freedom, both physical and mental. Their disregard for convention means that they are perceived as eccentric and idiosyncratic. This position can bring restlessness and a desire for constant excitement, and the subjects may thrive on chaos and upheaval. If this is the case, they may find it difficult to adapt to a routine existence. If Uranus is well aspected, these individuals will possess a streak of brilliance that could lead to them making important discoveries that will greatly benefit mankind. If Uranus is negatively aspected, nervous tension may result.

2 URANUS IN THE SECOND HOUSE

THIS IS THE HOUSE of money and investments. When Uranus shines from this position, these people often display an unpredictable attitude towards money, and rash investments may lead to financial problems. However, if a practical earth sign is emphasized in the chart, considerable financial gains could be made. If Uranus is

Music Stand
People with Uranus in the first house can possess a talent for making music.

Blackboard and Chalk
Children with Uranus in the third house are likely to display a precocious intelligence.

badly aspected by the Sun, Moon, or Venus, these subjects may be cool and distant, finding it difficult to show affection to their loved ones.

3 URANUS IN THE THIRD HOUSE

ALTHOUGH THEY ARE likely to have original and inventive minds combined with a fertile imagination, these people tend to make erratic progress both at school and work, for they find all forms of discipline different to tolerate. If Uranus is positively aspected, they will be cool-headed and logical. However, if the planet occupies a fixed sign or is negatively aspected, these people may be wilfully contrary and stubborn, a trait they must work hard to overcome.

4 URANUS IN THE FOURTH HOUSE

THOSE WITH URANUS in the fourth house may find that their desire for independence clashes with their need for a stable home, causing tension in romantic relationships. If Aries or Sagittarius are prominent in the chart, the longing for freedom will be increased, whereas Cancer or Pisces will encourage a love of the home. The subjects may have had an unsettled childhood, with many changes of address.

5 URANUS IN THE FIFTH HOUSE

THIS PLACING OFTEN indicates a string of whirlwind affairs with unsuitable partners. The subjects tend to display a somewhat reckless attitude towards affairs of the heart, plunging into new relationships without pausing to consider the consequences. Creative potential is greatly encouraged by this placing, and these people often make talented artists, actors, and musicians.

Quill Pen
Uranus in the fifth indicates creative talents.

Astronomical Equipment
Uranus in the tenth house
creates an interest in scientific
subjects such as astronomy.

6 URANUS IN THE SIXTH HOUSE

THOSE BORN WITH Uranus in the sixth house have a complex attitude towards work. This is the house of Virgo, which encourages steady and slow working habits, but the disruptive influence of Uranus means that these individuals soon become bored with routine tasks. A secure job with plenty of variety is the perfect solution. These people must learn to relax, since constant tension may cause health problems.

7 URANUS IN THE SEVENTH HOUSE

FROM THIS HOUSE, Uranus exerts a powerful influence on relationships, and this position is associated with constant romantic upheavals – spur-of-the-moment affairs and sudden separations. These people are free spirits. Their innate need for emotional freedom tends to cause problems when it comes to affairs of the heart. An open relationship suits these individuals best, but they may experience difficulties in finding a partner who is prepared to agree to such a permissive arrangement.

8 URANUS IN THE EIGHTH HOUSE

WHEN URANUS IS PLACED in the eighth house, a negligent, careless attitude to financial matters is very likely. These people are not usually materialistic, and financial security is not important to them. Indeed, if the subjects do unexpectedly inherit a fortune, they will probably give it all to charity. Sexual relationships may cause a few problems: these subjects possess fluctuating sexual appetites, passionate one moment, cool and detached the next. Their unfortunate partners may find this unpredictability difficult to tolerate.

9 URANUS IN THE NINTH HOUSE

PEOPLE WITH URANUS in the ninth house tend to be original and brilliant thinkers. Their strong powers of intelligence are formidable, and they often possess scientific flair or unique literary talents. Constant mental stimulation is necessary – these people reach out to unique and exciting experiences with both hands. Travel is important to these individuals, and they will enjoy exotic and unusual experiences while broadening their horizons.

10 URANUS IN THE TENTH HOUSE

THE TENTH HOUSE governs ambition and aspiration, and when Uranus is in this house it has a powerful influence on the career. These people will be attracted to unusual, ground-breaking work, perhaps in the space

Thermometer
Considerate and caring, those
born with Uranus in the
twelfth house excel
at ministering
to others.

industry or other scientific fields. Sudden changes of career may occur, and the subjects must make sure that they learn from their past jobs and accept all experience as beneficial. These individuals are strong-willed and ambitious, and will only be happy in a job with plenty of autonomy and responsibility.

11 URANUS IN THE ELEVENTH HOUSE

THIS IS THE AQUARIAN house, and the influence of Uranus is greatly increased here. Although always friendly and charming, these people need emotional privacy. This makes it difficult for them to form long-term romantic partnerships since they tend to fear that intimacy may threaten their solitude. However, they will enjoy a lively social life and possess a wide circle of friends and acquaintances. Esoteric hobbies and pastimes appeal to these individuals.

Aquarius Cigarette Card
Aquarius is the sign of
the zodiac traditionally
associated with Uranus.

12 URANUS IN THE TWELFTH HOUSE

URANUS IS A KINDLY and humanitarian planet, and the twelfth house represents charitable instincts. Consequently, these people have a very strong sense of altruistic duty, and will be prepared to make sacrifices for the good of others. Caring for their elderly relatives or dependants is very characteristic of these people, as is work in the caring professions. Although the subjects have a solicitous attitude towards humanity at large, they may find it very difficult to make a long-term emotional commitment to one other person.

PLANETS

SUN

MOON

MERCURY

VENUS

MARS

JUPITER

SATURN

♅
URANUS

NEPTUNE

PLUTO

SIGNS

♈
ARIES

♉
TAURUS

♊
GEMINI

♋
CANCER

♌
LEO

♍
VIRGO

♎
LIBRA

♏
SCORPIO

♐
SAGITTARIUS

♑
CAPRICORN

♒
AQUARIUS

♓
PISCES

NEPTUNE THROUGH THE HOUSES

Neptune can encourage idealism, imagination, and spirituality, but if negatively aspected may also bring a tendency towards carelessness, indecision, and escapism. The planet's house position indicates the area of life in which these characteristics will reveal themselves. For example, people with Neptune in the second house, the house of finance, are likely to possess a rather incompetent and disorganized attitude towards their financial affairs, frittering away their money or giving it to others. When the planet is afflicted, its house position indicates the areas in which these people may practise self-deception and escapist tendencies.

1 NEPTUNE IN THE FIRST HOUSE

NEPTUNE FROM THE first house tends to weaken the characteristics of the Ascendant. The planet brings a dreamy, impractical, and idealistic influence. These people shrink from the harsh realities of life and often seek refuge in a fantasy world. If Neptune is afflicted, they may even turn to drink and drugs as a form of escapism. This placing often brings an abundance of creative talent.

2 NEPTUNE IN THE SECOND HOUSE

IF NEPTUNE IS well aspected, these individuals will possess shrewd financial judgement and enjoy a large income. However, this placing also brings great generosity and extravagance, and a practical attitude to money should be encouraged. Happily, the planet's

Aromatherapy Massage Oils
People with Neptune in the sixth house are susceptible to stress. Massage may help to relieve their tension.

effect in the field of love is extremely positive. These people usually possess an imaginative attitude to romance, and make wonderful lovers.

3 NEPTUNE IN THE THIRD HOUSE

DREAMY AND PENSIVE, these people can often appear rather vague and unfocused. However, the third house is related to the mind, and in fact both the imagination and intuition will be sharpened by this placing of Neptune. As children, these people may have found it difficult to concentrate for more than a few moments. Their early education may have been problematic, with a series of disappointing exam results.

Sheet Music
Neptune in the third house can produce a particularly beautiful singing or speaking voice.

4 NEPTUNE IN THE FOURTH HOUSE

NEPTUNE IN THE fourth house indicates strong family ties. These people are likely to have enjoyed eventful and unconventional childhoods, and may still share a close emotional bond with their mothers. If the planet is badly aspected, there may be rather discordant family relationships and a chaotic, disorganized domestic environment.

5 NEPTUNE IN THE FIFTH HOUSE

PEOPLE WITH NEPTUNE in the fifth house will possess a dreamy and idealistic attitude towards romantic relationships. Their hearts rule their heads and they tend to plunge into relationships without sufficient thought. Disaster and heartbreak can be the result, and caution and practical common sense should be encouraged.

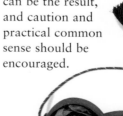

Chocolates
Neptune in the seventh house encourages a pleasure in giving.

Sidebar navigation:

PLANETS
SUN
MOON
MERCURY
VENUS
MARS
JUPITER
SATURN
URANUS
NEPTUNE
PLUTO

SIGNS
ARIES
TAURUS
GEMINI
CANCER
LEO
VIRGO
LIBRA
PISCES

Tarot Cards
Mystical forms of religion and esoteric practices are fascinating to people with Neptune in the ninth house.

6 NEPTUNE IN THE SIXTH HOUSE

THESE PEOPLE ARE often serious hypochondriacs, with an over-imaginative approach to their numerous ailments. It is true, however, that they are often allergic to certain foods. Alternative therapies may be the best solution. These individuals find it difficult to take a disciplined attitude to their work. They dislike strict routine and are often rather unreliable and erratic workers.

7 NEPTUNE IN THE SEVENTH HOUSE

THESE PEOPLE EITHER rush impetuously into a permanent relationship with insufficient forethought, or back away from a long-term commitment in fear of losing their independence. They are true romantics, and tend to ignore the boring practicalities of life. These individuals need a partner who will appreciate the romantic devotion they offer, yet encourage them to keep in touch with reality.

8 NEPTUNE IN THE EIGHTH HOUSE

THIS PLACING BRINGS an intense, smouldering sexuality, and the powers of seduction will be greatly increased. These people will possess magnetic powers of attraction and will never be without a string of admirers. As a result their sexuality needs positive expression and must not be suppressed. They tend to be financially generous, if rather gullible. Caution and professional financial advice are advisable.

9 NEPTUNE IN THE NINTH HOUSE

FROM THE NINTH house, Neptune brings an enlightened, philosophical outlook on life. These people will display a great interest in other religions and they are fascinated by esoteric or occult practices. Indeed, they must preserve a measure of scepticism to avoid being taken in by charlatans. These people often have very vivid dreams, and are likely to be extremely creative and imaginative.

Personal Stereo
People with Neptune in the twelfth enjoy solitary pursuits.

10 NEPTUNE IN THE TENTH HOUSE

WHEN NEPTUNE OCCUPIES the tenth house, the planet indicates a colourful career with several changes of direction. The subjects are intensely romantic, with a lively imagination. These are attractive attributes, but these individuals must try to keep at least one foot on the ground, instead of surrendering to fantasy. If Neptune is conjunct the Midheaven, the sign Neptune occupies must be carefully considered, as it will reveal the innermost aspirations and objectives of these people.

11 NEPTUNE IN THE ELEVENTH HOUSE

THIS PLANETARY PLACING indicates friendship and group participation. These people tend to be extremely sociable, and usually possess a wide circle of close friends and acquaintances. They are generous and supportive, and must beware of selfish friends who may try to take advantage of their kind and generous nature. These individuals have a caring and humanitarian streak in their characters, and are frequently involved in fund-raising for charity. They enjoy group activities, and are members of a variety of clubs and societies, particularly those with a charitable purpose.

12 NEPTUNE IN THE TWELFTH HOUSE

THIS IS THE Pisces/Neptune house, and the planet's influence is strong from here. Although Neptune works well from this position, it can also bring reclusive tendencies to the personality. These individuals have an intensely private and solitary side to their characters, and they will occasionally need to retreat from the stresses and strains of everyday life. They tend to shun the limelight and to work best in isolation, particularly if they are involved in creative work. They like to let their work speak for them, and are not comfortable with self-publicity. These individuals are ideally suited to a career in one of the caring professions, for they are intensely sympathetic to those in need.

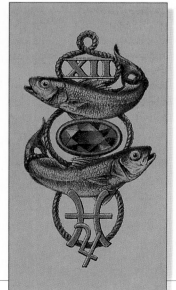

Pisces Cigarette Card
This card shows the symbol and glyph of Pisces, the sign ruled by the planet Neptune.

PLANETS

SUN

MOON

MERCURY

VENUS

MARS

JUPITER

SATURN

URANUS

Ψ
NEPTUNE

PLUTO

SIGNS

ARIES

TAURUS

GEMINI

CANCER

LEO

VIRGO

LIBRA

SCORPIO

SAGITTARIUS

CAPRICORN

AQUARIUS

PISCES

PLANETS
SUN
MOON
MERCURY
VENUS
MARS
JUPITER
SATURN
URANUS
NEPTUNE
PLUTO

SIGNS
ARIES
TAURUS
GEMINI
CANCER
LEO
VIRGO
LIBRA
SCORPIO
SAGITTARIUS
CAPRICORN
AQUARIUS
PISCES

PLUTO THROUGH THE HOUSES

Pluto is associated with the hidden depths of the subconscious, and its movements force buried problems and worries into the open. These can only be resolved through dramatic change and transformation. Therefore, the house in which Pluto falls may prove to be a source of difficulty. However, the planet can act as a purge, bringing concealed problems to the surface and eliminating them, and exerting a purifying and regenerative influence. Pluto is the ruler of Scorpio and is particularly influential for people with their Sun or Ascendant sign in Scorpio. The planet is at its most powerful when placed in the eighth (Scorpio) house.

1 PLUTO IN THE FIRST HOUSE

WHICHEVER SIGN PLUTO occupies, from this house the planet's influence will darken the personality. These people have an instinctive urge to explore every aspect of a situation or problem in depth. This tendency can be extremely useful in some jobs, but there is also a danger of becoming obsessive. Pluto in the first house heightens the emotions, and these individuals are likely to be extremely passionate and sensual. These people tend to be ambitious, and their emotional energy will also be channelled into their careers.

2 PLUTO IN THE SECOND HOUSE

A PASSIONATE SENSUALITY is typical of the second house, and people with this placing are skilled lovers. They are also shrewd business people, with plenty of financial acumen. A successful career is likely, although these individuals must be on their guard against becoming too greedy or materialistic. Possessiveness may be a problem, and these people will have to overcome a tendency to regard their partner as someone they own.

*Fingerprint
Spying and
investigation
fascinate
people with
Pluto in the
third house.*

*Indian
Perfume
Bottle
Pluto in the
second house
reveals an
appreciation
of beautiful
and unusual
objects.*

3 PLUTO IN THE THIRD HOUSE

PLUTO COUNSELS SECRECY while the third house encourages candour, and as a result these people may be torn between openness and silence. They will stop, look, and listen before committing themselves to anything, and while they may appear to be totally unaware of what is going on around them, in fact they will be busily amassing information for later use.

4 PLUTO IN THE FOURTH HOUSE

THIS IS NOT AN EASY PLACING for Pluto, and may indicate a difficult childhood. The parents may have been distant and unloving, or repressive disciplinarians. In an attempt to compensate for their unhappy childhood, these people will be eager to create a close and secure domestic scene, but must beware of becoming too possessive of their loved ones.

5 PLUTO IN THE FIFTH HOUSE

PEOPLE WITH PLUTO in the fifth house are subject to intense and powerful emotions. They are likely to enjoy a passionate and eventful love life, with an above-average number of love affairs, and may find it difficult to form a stable long-term partnership. These people possess an abundance of creative ability, and are often talented writers, artists, and musicians. Their creative powers may even be channelled into producing a large family of talented children.

*Cupid
Pluto in the fifth
house intensifies
romantic leanings
in the personality.*

6 PLUTO IN THE SIXTH HOUSE

THESE PEOPLE ARE all too ready to drive themselves into the ground in the pursuit of excellence. Industrious and hard-working, they possess tremendous powers of self-discipline, and can become quite obsessive about adhering to a strict routine. If Pluto is well aspected, these people will be able to focus their abundant energy positively, and their already formidable powers of concentration will be even further enhanced. If Pluto is negatively aspected, suppressed stress and tension may cause various health problems.

7 PLUTO IN THE SEVENTH HOUSE

PEOPLE WITH PLUTO in the seventh house will want to be the dominant partner in their emotional relationships as well as their business partnerships. Indeed, they may even unconsciously seek out a weaker partner, in order to ensure that they are completely in control of the relationship. These individuals possess sound financial skills, and Pluto works well from this house for business partnerships but less positively for emotional relationships. Much energy and emotion will be invested in a loving relationship, which will have some marvellous moments but also some very rocky patches. Any problems must be addressed and worked though, not swept under the carpet.

8 PLUTO IN THE EIGHTH HOUSE

WHEN PLUTO OCCUPIES the eighth house, intuition and logic will be happily combined. As a result, these people usually possess a shrewd business head, especially if the planet occupies Cancer or Virgo. This is the Scorpio/Pluto house, and the emotional level will be particularly high. However, the influence of Pluto may cause some repression, and sexual expression in

Scorpio Cigarette Card
This card depicts the symbol and glyph of Scorpio, which is ruled by Pluto.

particular may be blocked. Although these people can be very secretive, any emotional problems will only be resolved by discussion with their partner.

9 PLUTO IN THE NINTH HOUSE

INTELLECTUAL processes are emphasized by this position, and these individuals have an innate desire to study and increase their intellectual horizons. They are true perfectionists and will often have difficulty in finishing a job, always believing that the result could be improved upon. These people also tend to possess strong spiritual and religious principles, and if Pluto is afflicted, they can become quite fanatical about their beliefs.

10 PLUTO IN THE TENTH HOUSE

THOSE WITH Pluto in the tenth house tend to be passionately involved in their careers. They work hard and are likely to enjoy great success. However, self-centred personal ambitions may encourage these people to trample on others in their eagerness to reach the top, and they must beware of becoming too ruthless and manipulative. These individuals must also recognize that their unceasing pursuit of success may cause them to neglect their family and friends, thus endangering their close relationships.

Solitaire
People with Pluto in the ninth house enjoy challenging games and puzzles.

11 PLUTO IN THE ELEVENTH HOUSE

PEOPLE WITH PLUTO in the eleventh house are sociable and gregarious and enjoy team activities. They eagerly seek the approval and good opinion of others, and the prospect of displeasing or disappointing their friends will cause them great alarm. This eagerness to please should not be allowed to get out of hand, since individuals may begin to live their lives solely to please others instead of themselves. Subjects possess a broad humanitarian streak, and if Pluto is positively aspected they will devote much time and effort to making the world a better place, possibly by joining charitable organizations and raising money to help those in need.

12 PLUTO IN THE TWELFTH HOUSE

PLUTO IN THE TWELFTH house will have a powerful effect on the unconscious, and these people are secretive, intense, and solitary. Their air of mystery will intrigue others, and they may have a string of admirers, but their inability to express their deepest thoughts and emotions will lead to unsatisfactory relationships. These people have an inquisitive streak, and are fascinated by espionage and investigative work. However, if this curious streak is turned inwards, they can become very introspective and self-obsessed.

Crown
Pluto in the tenth house signals a love of power, especially if Pluto occupies Leo.

PLANETS

SUN

MOON

MERCURY

VENUS

MARS

JUPITER

SATURN

URANUS

NEPTUNE

♇
PLUTO

SIGNS

♈
ARIES

♉
TAURUS

♊
GEMINI

♋
CANCER

♌
LEO

♍
VIRGO

♎
LIBRA

♏
SCORPIO

THE
ASPECTS

Certain angles between planets in a birth chart are known as "aspects". One planet is "in aspect" to another if the angle between them is of a specific number of degrees, counted round the circumference of the chart. The acetate overlay in this pack should make it easy for you to discover which of the planets in your chart are in aspect. If planets are in conjunction, they are within 9° of each other, and their qualities will often combine in a mutually beneficial way. Sextiles (planets 60° apart) and trines (120° apart), are considered positive aspects, while squares (90° apart) and oppositions (180° apart) are negative aspects. Note that positive aspects are not always agreeable, and not all negative aspects are necessarily adverse.

One of a series of astrological maps drawn by Andreas Cellarius in 1660.

PLANETS

☉
SUN

MOON

MERCURY

VENUS

MARS

JUPITER

SATURN

URANUS

NEPTUNE

PLUTO

SIGNS

♈
ARIES

♉
TAURUS

♊
GEMINI

♋
CANCER

♌
LEO

♍
VIRGO

♎
LIBRA

♏
SCORPIO

♐
SAGITTARIUS

♑
CAPRICORN

♒
AQUARIUS

♓
PISCES

THE ASPECTS OF THE SUN

The aspects made by the Sun to other planets and to the Ascendant and the Midheaven are extremely important in interpreting a birth chart. Astrologers allow an orb of influence for a planetary aspect, when it is not precise to a degree. We have expressed suggested orbs in the colour system used in the planetary tables supplied with this pack. It is necessary to assess the importance of each aspect. One between the Sun and the Moon is particularly important since the subject's self-expression (Sun) and instincts (Moon) will be influenced. Aspects may complement, or conflict with, Sun-sign characteristics.

THE SUN'S ASPECTS TO THE MOON

Without an ephemeris it is impossible to know the exact position of the Moon at your birth. Therefore, in reading the Sun's aspects to the Moon, you can ignore the rules concerning the placing of the planets in the three shades of colour in the signs, and rely on the sign placing. For instance, if the Sun is in Gemini and the Moon is in Aquarius, call it a trine aspect. If the Sun is in Scorpio and the Moon is in Leo, call it a square aspect.

Conjunction This important aspect occurs when the subject is born near the time of the New Moon. It means that the Sun and Moon are likely to fall in the same sign and house, and the effect of this is to strengthen the typical Sun-sign characteristics of the individual. Instinctive and intuitive reactions, which are usually influenced and guided by the Moon, will be affected by this conjunction, and the person is likely to react to emotional situations in the manner of the Sun sign. Emotional impulsiveness can be a problem, because the will is likely to overwhelm the feelings.

You must also consider the house occupied by this aspect, as the area of life it influences will be dealt with in the manner of the Sun sign rather than the Moon, and if either Mercury or Venus is also in the same sign, the Sun-sign characteristics will be so heavily emphasized that the subject is almost a caricature of the Sun sign.

Cosmic Influences
Astrologers believe that each zodiacal sign has influence over a specific area of our bodies.

Positive aspects When the Sun makes positive aspects to the Moon it helps to integrate a personality. If there is a trine aspect, and the two planets concerned are of the same element, the flow of enthusiasm (fire), practicality (earth), intellectual ability (air), or emotion (water) will be strong and positive. The instincts and reactions that are dictated by the Moon should integrate well with the characteristics shown by the Sun. The sextile has a much less powerful integrating effect. Its influence tends to merely emphasize the extrovert tendencies from positive signs or the introvert ones from negative signs.

Negative aspects People with negative Sun/Moon aspects tend to be restless and somewhat discontent with their life; their moods change easily, and their inability to feel content with life can cause difficulties in emotional relationships. The opposition (which occurs when one is born at the time of the Full Moon) causes a polarity between the subject's conscious will and unconscious mind, leading to unexplained conflict and tension. The square aspect accents the quality (or quadruplicity) of the occupied signs, and makes a person more outgoing (cardinal), stubborn (fixed), or flexible (mutable). A tendency to worry unnecessarily, and to be physically and emotionally restless, can lead to minor health problems.

THE SUN'S ASPECTS TO MERCURY

Mercury cannot be more than 28° from the Sun, so the only aspect that can be formed between the two is a conjunction (or a minor semi-sextile, a very subtle aspect). If the two planets occupy the same sign, the individual will think in the manner of the Sun sign, but if Mercury falls in the preceding or following sign, the mind will work in the manner of that sign. If the Sun and Mercury relationship form a conjunction, this aspect suggests that the individual will be a slow developer, who will be optimistic, enthusiastic, and eager for material progress.

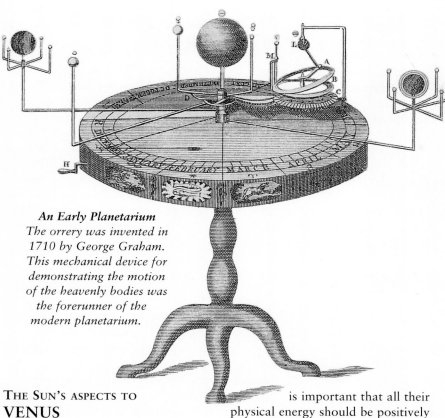

An Early Planetarium
The orrery was invented in
1710 by George Graham.
This mechanical device for
demonstrating the motion
of the heavenly bodies was
the forerunner of the
modern planetarium.

THE SUN'S ASPECTS TO
VENUS

Like Mercury, the only aspect that Venus can form to the Sun is the conjunction (or the minor aspects, the semi-sextile and semi-square). If there is a conjunction between the two planets, this will encourage displays of love and affection; the attitude to financial matters will be shown by the Sun sign but strengthened by this aspect. These people enjoy the good life, sometimes to the point of self-indulgence, but the blending of powerful solar vitality with Venusian sympathy and the need to relate usually make them positive and happy, with easy-going charm.

If the conjunction is afflicted by an opposition or square from the Moon or Saturn, there may be elements of disappointment and unhappiness in the emotional life.

THE SUN'S ASPECTS TO
MARS

Conjunction The physical energy that Mars adds to the vitality of the Sun makes these individuals powerful, forceful people, and it is important that all their physical energy should be positively channelled – perhaps in heavy sport, regular exercise, or hard manual work. They will have plenty of strength and often a wiry, athletic frame. They should nevertheless be careful not to push themselves too hard and ensure that they take time to relax. This aspect can strengthen the emotional energy, and if the planets are in a water sign, the energy may be expressed through devotion to a good cause or an ideal.

These subjects can be selfish, and because Mars rules Aries, the Arien will to win is likely to show itself. There may be a tendency to suffer with headaches, and through undue haste these people may be accident-prone. Daring and bravery are very common, often to the point of heroism, but they should make sure that risk-taking is not foolhardiness.

Positive aspects Many of the characteristics of the conjunction will be seen in the trine and sextile, but will not be so rashly expressed. The resources of energy are likely to be controlled and hastiness reduced. The individual's energy will be vigorous and well focused.

Negative aspects Overwork may lead to strain and tension, which will be expressed in sudden outbursts of anger and spleen. It is only if the tendency is recognized and can be controlled that the additional energy offered by these aspects of Sun and Mars can be positively used.

Where the love life is concerned, it is important that these people have co-operation and enthusiasm from their partner, otherwise the ensuing frustration can lead to a fiery temper that will need to be kept well under control.

THE SUN'S ASPECTS TO
JUPITER

Conjunction Traditionally, this is considered a fortunate aspect, and it often seems to be the case that people with this aspect have a fair amount of good luck. Maybe this is because the aspect makes them optimistic and warm, with an excellent sense of humour, a philosophical outlook on life, and an apparently instinctive way of finding money when they need it. They have first-rate minds and no lack of ambition, although they will not use ruthlessness to achieve their ends. They enjoy good food and drink, and as a result sometimes suffer from indigestion and can also become overweight.

Positive aspects As is often the case, these aspects have a similar effect to the conjunction, together with an additional impulse to use the energies to broaden the mind and expand the intellect. If Venus is also well placed, the tendency to enjoy life is emphasized, and the outlook will be positive and optimistic. There may be an interest in either the law or publishing, and reading is likely to be a major form of relaxation. If a flair for teaching is suggested elsewhere in the birth chart, a positive aspect between the Sun and Jupiter will encourage it. These subjects are not particularly competitive, but they will enjoy intellectual board games such as chess and backgammon.

PLANETS

SUN

MOON

MERCURY

VENUS

MARS

JUPITER

SATURN

URANUS

NEPTUNE

PLUTO

SIGNS

ARIES

TAURUS

GEMINI

CANCER

LEO

VIRGO

LIBRA

SCORPIO

SAGITTARIUS

CAPRICORN

AQUARIUS

PISCES

PLANETS
SUN
MOON
MERCURY
VENUS
MARS
JUPITER
SATURN
URANUS
NEPTUNE
PLUTO
SIGNS
ARIES
TAURUS
GEMINI
CANCER
LEO
VIRGO
LIBRA
SCORPIO
SAGITTARIUS
CAPRICORN
AQUARIUS
PISCES

Negative aspects These people will have a tendency to exaggerate and can all too easily lose their sense of perspective. Seeing the broad sweep of a concept, they do not have the desire to examine it minutely, and small detail is often ignored. If they can recognize this element of their personality, they may be able to avoid the accompanying problems.

These subjects lack moderation and, if drawn to gambling (including taking risks in investment), can easily be carried away. Any tendency towards negative escapism through drink or drugs should be carefully watched. If several planets in the chart are in earth signs, the negative effect of these aspects is likely to be weakened, and the jovial side of Jupiter will show itself positively.

THE SUN'S ASPECTS TO
SATURN

Conjunction This conjunction will be a strong focal point in the birth chart. The Sun and Saturn are traditionally considered "enemies" because the Sun provides vitality while Saturn restrains it. When they are in conjunction, we find the Sun's activity at best channelled and at worst restrained by the powerful intervention of Saturn. If most of the aspects from the other planets are positive, the worst Saturn will be able to do is act as a constraint,

and it can even be a stabilizer. For instance, if the Sun is in a fire sign, its influence will be steadied and its more extreme activities restrained. If the conjunction is in Capricorn (which is ruled by Saturn), the qualities attributed to that sign will be enhanced. People with this conjunction will be somewhat shy and unconfident, especially when young; later they may come to terms with their shyness as ambition and determination take over. Steady exercise is recommended because rheumatic problems may arise.

Positive aspects Common sense and a practical, restrained outlook are signified by positive aspects between the Sun and Saturn. On occasion, enthusiasm is restricted, especially when these people are faced with challenging situations, although this should not be a problem unless shyness and lack of self-confidence are suggested elsewhere in the chart. Positive aspects between the Sun and Saturn aid the achievement of ambitions. These are cautious and circumspect individuals who take risks only after careful deliberation.

Negative aspects These aspects can be thoroughly limiting. Confidence is undermined, and if the individual's parents were unsympathetic or over-critical, there will be debilitating feelings of inadequacy. Sometimes the health can also be undermined, with a ready tendency to catch colds and chills that are exacerbated by aches and pains. The square is more inhibiting than the opposition, the latter providing stability and restraint and injecting common sense.

Heavenly Bodies
In the 14th century, when the heavens were thought to influence the body, astrologers ascertained the state of the monarch's health.

THE SUN'S ASPECTS TO
URANUS

Conjunction Rebelliousness, eccentricity, and unpredictability are qualities to be expected from this powerful conjunction, but it can also be a highly positive force, bestowing scientific ability and creative flair. The driving force of these personalities is very strong indeed, especially if the conjunction receives aspects from Mars or Pluto, or if both the Sun and Uranus are in the tenth house. Restraint and control will need to be cultivated – consider the position of Saturn to see if it offers a steadying influence.

Positive aspects If a birth chart contains a trine or sextile from Uranus to the Sun, the personality will be spiced with originality and will possess a degree of magnetism. If Venus is well placed, dynamic sexual attraction will be evident. If the Sun is in an extrovert sign, such as Leo or Sagittarius, powers of leadership and popularity will be enhanced. Emotional and nervous energy are augmented, and will be positively exploited. Positive aspects, especially the trine, will contribute alertness and an enthusiastic driving force to the individual, but these characteristics can be expressed in an unpredictable manner.

Negative aspects Perversity, stubbornness, and other negative traits are often present, especially with a square aspect. Self-willed behaviour can cause problems. Periods of tension may occur, and the individual will be "difficult" from time to time, although other indications in the birth chart may mitigate the influence. If the subject can develop the humanitarian side of Uranus, rather than the perverse and stubborn, these powerful planetary forces can be beneficial. Sun and Uranus aspects can sometimes affect sexual behaviour, more usually in men than women. The square, in particular, has been said to indicate homosexuality.

THE SUN'S ASPECTS TO
NEPTUNE

Conjunction This conjunction may cause the individual to be sensitive, highly intuitive, and imaginative. The characteristics of the Sun sign will be softened if Neptune occupies the same sign. Provided that the conjunction is free from negative aspects, from the Moon or Mars in particular, the imagination will be creatively expressed, but interest in the occult should be carefully governed. If the conjunction is in opposition or square aspect to the Moon, there may a dangerous desire for negative escapism.

Positive aspects Intuition is keen and these people will have a highly inspirational imagination – but they may be far too lackadaisical to take advantage of it. Daydreaming results in positive creative potential being wasted, and there is often an inability to tackle hard work.

Negative aspects Faced with difficulties, people with negative aspects of the Sun and Neptune can all too easily take refuge in escapist behaviour, and may rely on alcohol, tobacco, and other forms of drugs for relief from their problems. This is most likely when Neptune is in either Libra or Scorpio, when there is a high probability that even medically administered drugs will react negatively on the system. Moderation, and the control of all escapist behaviour patterns and the faults described above, are essential.

THE SUN'S ASPECTS TO
PLUTO

Conjunction Individuals with this conjunction have a need to explore their innermost nature, and they like to analyze their every inclination and decision. This will be the case particularly if the aspect falls in Cancer or Scorpio, in which case any tendency towards introspection or obsessive analysis will need to be opposed. If the conjunction appears in Leo, subjects may seek to exert power over others; in Virgo, they will wish to lead others. In all cases their behaviour tends to be extreme, and this aspect in a chart can even indicate political fanaticism.

Positive aspects An ability to self-analyse is usually present and will lead to psychological growth. The need to explore every aspect of a situation often translates into a real talent for research, and if medical ability is indicated elsewhere in the chart, these aspects will help someone interested in psychiatry or psychology.

Negative aspects These tend to inhibit the subjects' ability to open up to others. Psychological blockage can often occur, and these people will sometimes suffer from physical constipation, too, which they worry about and exacerbate. It is possible that a tendency towards obsessive behaviour will be present, but this can be counteracted by a Geminian influence elsewhere in the chart, and Venus in one of its own signs, or receiving a trine from the Moon, will induce a relaxed attitude.

THE SUN'S ASPECTS TO
THE ASCENDANT

Conjunction If the Sun falls in the first house, the individual will be well integrated psychologically, and the strength of the Ascendant and Sun signs will be considerable. If they fall in the same sign, the subject is known as a "double Gemini" or whatever the Sun sign is. This aspect brings a sunny and positive outlook, but a negative aspect from Saturn will weaken the effect, and one from Jupiter can cause the individual to be somewhat overbearing.

Positive aspects The house position of the Sun will be a focal point of the chart, and there will be unity between the Sun and Ascendant. The most potent influence is a trine with the Sun in the fifth house, when fifth house matters – creativity, pleasure, love – will be positively emphasized.

Life Force
Although the Sun is actually a star, astrologers consider it the most important planet in our birth chart.

Negative aspects The house position is particularly significant in the case of negative aspects to the Ascendant. An opposition from the sixth house may be a potential source of strain on the subject's health, although if the Sun is well aspected by the Moon or Mars the placing can be invigorating. A square from the fourth house suggests domestic upheaval, possibly problems with parents. A square from the tenth house shows a strong driving force and a desire for worldly progress.

THE SUN'S ASPECTS TO
THE MIDHEAVEN

Conjunction The individual will have been born around noon, and all the solar energy and drive will be channelled into achieving ambitions and aspirations. These people are self-confident but must take care to control pomposity and arrogance.

Positive aspects These subjects will identify strongly with the qualities of the sign on the Midheaven and aspire to them; ambition will be pursued but without ruthlessness.

Negative aspects It may be hard for the subject to achieve objectives and express the qualities of the Midheaven sign in a positive way. Fulfilment will come through effort.

PLANETS

SUN

MOON

MERCURY

VENUS

MARS

JUPITER

SATURN

URANUS

NEPTUNE

PLUTO

SIGNS

ARIES

TAURUS

GEMINI

CANCER

LEO

VIRGO

LIBRA

SCORPIO

SAGITTARIUS

CAPRICORN

AQUARIUS

PISCES

PLANETS

SUN

☽
MOON

MERCURY

VENUS

MARS

JUPITER

SATURN

URANUS

NEPTUNE

PLUTO

SIGNS

♈
ARIES

♉
TAURUS

♊
GEMINI

♋
CANCER

♌
LEO

♍
VIRGO

♎
LIBRA

♏
SCORPIO

♐
SAGITTARIUS

♑
CAPRICORN

♒
AQUARIUS

♓
PISCES

THE INFLUENCE OF THE MOON

The Moon circles the zodiac approximately once every twenty-eight days, taking only two and a half days to travel through each sign. Unfortunately, we do not have sufficient room in this pack to give the Moon's position for every hour of every day. However, with the tables provided you can discover which sign the Moon is in, the degree the Moon falls on is needed to calculate its aspects. An ephemeris for the year of your birth will show the position of the Moon throughout that year and its precise position in the sky at the time you were born.

THE INFLUENCE OF
THE MOON

Together with the Sun and the Ascendant, the Moon is one of the most important factors in the birth chart, and its influence on us is deeply personal. For an interpretation of the Moon through the signs, see pages 20–23. The Moon indicates the way we respond to all situations in life and is thought to influence our moods. Its position in your birth chart will reveal whether you take a level approach to life or whether you have mood swings and suffer from emotional extremes of elation and depression.

The Moon represents the mother, but modern astrological research suggests that the Moon shows us the mother not as she actually is, but as she is perceived by her son or daughter. For instance, a subject who has the Moon in Taurus may well think of his or her mother as possessive, but the mother's own birth chart may reveal that she is emotionally cool.

The Moon also influences the characteristics that we inherit from our parents and ancestors, and it is as well to consider this when assessing any problems that a subject may be experiencing. It is often the case that a subject is unaware of the instincts and motivation that cause a particular line of action to be taken.

The Power of the Moon
The waxing and waning of the Moon is thought to affect our moods and emotions.

The sign and house position of the Moon can give us clues about the way in which we are influenced by our family background, and by our mother in particular.

Perhaps the most important lunar influence is on our emotions, and again, according to the sign occupied by the Moon, we can judge our emotional level. For instance, people with the Moon in Capricorn will appear unemotional, although in actual fact they are simply much less inclined than other people to show their true feelings. Someone with a Gemini Moon may rationalize their emotions, and by intellectualizing them unduly curtail their emotional reactions to situations – reactions that are honest and forthright, and need to be expressed. In contrast, someone with the Moon in a fire sign will have "fiery" emotions – of joy, happiness, enthusiasm, or even anger – that will tend to flair up very quickly. Whether those emotions are sustained or fizzle out will depend on the fire sign in which the Moon resides.

The Moon is at its most powerful when it is placed in Cancer, because this is the sign it rules. With this placing in a birth chart, its influence will vie in strength with that of the Sun, and Cancerian characteristics are likely to be quite strongly marked. The Moon's power is also enhanced when it falls in the Cancerian house – the fourth house of the birth chart. Here, everything related to the fourth house, such as heredity and home, will be of increased importance to the subject. You should also take special note of the influence of the Moon if it is placed in the first house, and the closer it is to the Ascendant the more powerful its influence will be. Whatever sign it is in, the Moon from the first house will exert a strong Cancerian influence on the personality of the individual.

If the Moon appears to be in the first house in a birth chart, it will need to be emphasized when you make your interpretation. If there is any doubt about the accuracy of the time of birth it is important to ascertain if the Moon is in the first or the twelfth house. To do this, you may have to ask your subject some searching questions. If they appear not to have the characteristics we describe for the Moon in the first house – if they are slightly shy, enjoy working behind the scenes, and are quite happy not to show off in any way, preferring to allow their work to speak for them – then the Moon is more likely to occupy the twelfth house of the horoscope.

When the Moon occupies the same sign as the Midheaven, there is excellent career potential. It is often the case that these individuals are in charge of large groups of people, and it is a common placing in the charts of conductors of orchestras, people in charge of big businesses, and politicians. See the Moon in the Tenth House, on page 57.

A calendar or diary for your year of birth can tell you whether you were born at the time of the New or Full Moon – or you can consult the Moon tables provided. If you were born with the Sun and Moon in the same sign, then you will have been born at the time of the New Moon. This means that you will not only have the personality characteristics of the sign through the influence of the Sun, you will also have the emotional level of the sign. In other words, you will react and respond intuitively and emotionally in the manner of the Sun sign because of the lunar influence. If you can discover the exact degree of the Moon and Sun using an ephemeris, you will discover if they are in conjunction. If this is the case, the double influence is even stronger.

If you were born when the Moon was full, the Sun and Moon were in opposite or "polar" signs across the zodiac – for instance, if the Moon is in Aries, the Sun will be in Libra. This often puts the Sun and Moon in an opposition aspect. In addition to the two different respective influences of the planets, you should consider whether there is a tendency to

suffer from inner restlessness or a certain element of discontent in the personality. Feelings of confusion and discontent are common with this particular placing, because the instincts bestowed by the Sun and Moon often disagree, and may pull the subject in different directions. This is also true to a lesser extent for those who are born at the time of the Moon's first and third quarter – a detailed calculation might show that the Sun and Moon are forming square aspects to each other.

Without an ephemeris you cannot be certain of the accuracy of your lunar aspects, and it would not be wise at this level to emphasize them in your interpretation. However, to make a general interpretation of the Moon's aspects, you can rely on the sign placing. For instance, if the Sun is in Gemini and the Moon is in Aquarius, they are four signs apart, approximately 120° away, which is a trine aspect. If the Sun is in Scorpio and the Moon is in Leo, they would be in a square aspect. To confirm whether the Moon is truly aspected to another planet, you will need to look at an ephemeris to check the exact position of the Moon in the birth chart. To find an interpretation of the Moon's aspects to the Sun, read the section on the Sun's aspects to the Moon on page 76. The brief list that follows explains the possible characteristics that will emerge when the Moon is in aspect to the other planets:

Moon to Mercury
Positive aspects can bestow shrewdness as well as an excellent memory. Negative aspects suggest a sarcastic tongue and a love of gossip.

Crayfish
On the façade of Notre Dame Cathedral in Paris is this 13th-century carving of Cancer as a crayfish. Cancer is now symbolized by the Crab.

Moon to Venus Natural charm and sensitivity are bestowed by positive aspects; squares and oppositions suggest problems with relationships.
Moon to Mars Good for vitality and robustness, unless the aspect is negative, when impulsiveness and a hot, quick temper may occur.
Moon to Jupiter Positive aspects bring kindness and sympathy, but negative ones cause the subject to dramatize and over-react to situations.
Moon to Saturn Common sense and a cautious outlook come with positive aspects, but there will be a tendency to succumb to depression if aspects are negative.
Moon to Uranus Mental originality and even brilliance are contributed by positive aspects, but negative aspects can cause nervous tension.
Moon to Neptune Positive aspects can aid imagination and idealism, but negative ones make the subject unworldly and sometimes escapist.
Moon to Pluto Positive aspects bring a need to get to the root of every problem, but negative aspects can cause obsessive tendencies.

PLANETS

SUN

MOON

MERCURY

VENUS

MARS

JUPITER

SATURN

URANUS

NEPTUNE

PLUTO

SIGNS

ARIES

TAURUS

GEMINI

CANCER

LEO

VIRGO

LIBRA

SCORPIO

SAGITTARIUS

CAPRICORN

AQUARIUS

PISCES

THE ASPECTS OF MERCURY

Aspects of Mercury are as important to the birth chart as the sign and house in which the planet falls. Mercury is thought to influence our intellect and communication skills. The sign in which it falls will reflect how we communicate, the house position will tell us in what area of life we are most likely to apply our mental powers, while the aspects to Mercury refine this information and reveal what other influences there will be in our way of thinking. Mercury intellectualizes any planet that it aspects, and even negative aspects sharpen the receiving planet, although they can cause tension and stress.

For Mercury's aspects to the Sun see the Sun's aspects to Mercury, page 76.
For Mercury's aspects to the Moon see page 81.

MERCURY'S ASPECTS TO
VENUS

Conjunction This is a good aspect for emotional relationships because it encourages a very loving and sympathetic nature. It also suggests empathy with colleagues and friends. There will be good communication skills, and the quick wits of Mercury work well with the emotions of Venus.

Other aspects Mercury and Venus can never be more than 76° apart, therefore they can form only a conjunction and sextile (or a semi-sextile or semi-square, minor aspects that we do not deal with here). The sextile aspect suggests friendliness and affection, and if the subject is creative, a considerable ability for craftwork. If Mercury or Venus are in earth signs, the love of natural materials such as wood, wool, and stone will be emphasized.

MERCURY'S ASPECTS TO
MARS

Conjunction This aspect indicates hard-working, assertive, competitive people with quick-thinking minds, capable of keeping well ahead of rivals in business or sport. There is sometimes a liking for satire and a humorous turn of mind. If there is aggression shown elsewhere in the

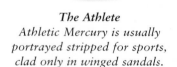

The Athlete
Athletic Mercury is usually portrayed stripped for sports, clad only in winged sandals.

chart, this aspect will sharpen it into a tendency to quarrel, or at least to voice opinions forcefully.

Positive aspects These aspects possess much the same qualities as the conjunction, but they also strengthen the nervous system, and allow the subject to act positively when the going gets rough and to deal with problems that might defeat others. Individuals with positive aspects between Mercury and Mars will positively thrive in a contentious atmosphere.

Negative aspects There is a strong likelihood of premature action and snap decisions being made without due consideration of a situation. Look elsewhere in the horoscope for indications of common sense and mental stability. The Sun or rising sign being an earth sign will help, as will a well-aspected Saturn. Tension may build up due to overwork, and if Mercury or Mars makes negative aspects to Uranus, illness due to mental strain is possible.

MERCURY'S ASPECTS TO
JUPITER

Conjunction A conjunction between Mercury and Jupiter will be helpful if the subject is interested in any kind of literary work, or indeed in science or mathematics, for it can bestow great intellectual potential. It is important to consider the sign and house placing, because they indicate how the mental energy is expressed, and what the intellectual outlook and attitude will be.

Positive aspects These suggest very good-natured and optimistic individuals who will have a high level of intellectual potential. This may not always be explored because their over-philosophical outlook can cause them to be too laid-back. These subjects would be wise to cultivate mental challenges in order to keep their minds active.

Negative aspects Individuals with negative aspects between Mercury and Jupiter often tend to be rather absent-minded, although there is good intellectual potential. They have a tendency to be sceptical and occasionally to exaggerate, which may cause complications. If Mercury or Jupiter is negatively aspected by Uranus, or if Mercury is in Virgo, there can be problems with the nervous system, and if biliousness is shown elsewhere in the horoscope this aspect can exacerbate it. Special care should be taken when signing documents, because these people often ignore the small print.

PLANETS

SUN

MOON

MERCURY

VENUS

MARS

JUPITER

SATURN

URANUS

NEPTUNE

PLUTO

SIGNS

ARIES

TAURUS

GEMINI

CANCER

LEO

VIRGO

LIBRA

SCORPIO

SAGITTARIUS

CAPRICORN

AQUARIUS

PISCES

MERCURY'S ASPECTS TO
SATURN

Conjunction A powerful aspect that bestows a serious outlook, good powers of concentration and perception, and the ability for practical thought. The mind works meticulously and cautiously, but the individual will on the whole be somewhat pessimistic, and if Mercury is a personal planet there can even be a love of solitude. If the conjunction is in a fire or an air sign it acts as a stabilizer to fiery energy and airy, lively intellectuality. In a water sign, it calms the emotions; in an earth sign, it suggests a degree of obstinacy and self-will.

Positive aspects Trines and sextiles between Mercury and Saturn denote a lively, positive individual who is extremely reliable. The subject is able to think in a very methodical and precise manner, and will be able to communicate clearly and precisely.

Negative aspects These individuals will have a passion for neatness and order that can become obsessive; they are often extremely hard on themselves and highly critical of others. They have a puritanical frame of mind and can be easily shocked. Pessimism and depression can occur, especially if the Moon and Saturn also form a negative aspect to each other. Suspicion and cunning are other possible traits, and sometimes these people are rather shy and lack self-confidence, especially at large social gatherings.

MERCURY'S ASPECTS TO
URANUS

Conjunction Someone with this aspect may well be a very private person, eager to go his or her own way, uninhibited by the demands of others. This is a dynamic influence that brings originality and brilliance of mind. Stubbornness and wilfulness may be also be apparent, especially if those characteristics are shown elsewhere in the horoscope.

The positive elements of this aspect should be encouraged, because at its best it can work wonderfully well.

Positive aspects Originality and bright ideas spring from unusual interests and a talent for exploiting them. An inventive imagination will add spice to creative or scientific work. If Leo or Jupiter is prominent in the birth chart, there will be a strong sense of drama, whereas if the subject has Mercury or Uranus as a personal planet, or if Mercury is in the same sign as the Sun, independence will be highly valued.

Negative aspects The same bright originality will be seen as with positive aspects, but there may be some nervous tension, especially if Mars is negatively aspected to Mercury or Uranus. These subjects have a tendency to speak without thinking, and are often rather caustic. They need to be aware of this and try to avoid hurting others' feelings. If Neptune receives negative aspects from the Sun or Moon, or squares the Ascendant, the individual may be under the delusion that he or she has special gifts that might save mankind.

Note: Aspects between Mercury and Uranus are often found in the charts of professional astrologers.

MERCURY'S ASPECTS TO
NEPTUNE

Conjunction This can be a delightful influence, provided it is kept under control. It is not an aspect that will aid common sense, and while the mental attributes of Mercury combined with the imagination and

The Twins
Mercury is the ruler of both Gemini and Virgo, and the two signs share a love of mental reasoning and communication.

inspiration of Neptune can result in an extremely interesting personality, he or she will be likely to drift off into daydreams or a private fantasy world. If the conjunction falls in Libra or Scorpio, the imagination may centre on romantic or sexual fantasies, respectively. Should it fall in Leo, Virgo, or Sagittarius, the results will be positive, and intellect and imagination will find expression through some form of creativity. Increased sensitivity and intuition may be marked if they are shown in other areas of the chart, and if psychic powers are indicated they will be strengthened by this aspect.

Positive aspects The effect of trines and sextiles between these two planets is similar to that of the conjunction, but the subject is likely to be more gentle and sensitive, instinctively knowing what friends and lovers are thinking. As with the conjunction, the world of the occult may attract, but this should be confirmed by the other aspects that Neptune receives.

Negative aspects If either planet is personal there may be a tendency towards self-deception, with the subject being unwilling to face facts. If the Sun is in Pisces, which is ruled by Neptune, the tendency to deceive may be a problem. If the Sun, Moon, or Ascendant falls in an earth sign, or if Saturn makes a positive aspect to them, this will indicate a practicality that can combat the deceptiveness.

PLANETS

SUN

MOON

MERCURY

VENUS

MARS

JUPITER

SATURN

URANUS

NEPTUNE

PLUTO

SIGNS

ARIES

TAURUS

GEMINI

CANCER

LEO

VIRGO

LIBRA

SCORPIO

SAGITTARIUS

CAPRICORN

AQUARIUS

PISCES

MERCURY'S ASPECTS TO
PLUTO

Conjunction   These people have sleuth-like minds and may be suited to a career either in investigation or research. They have the ability to think deeply and intuitively, and are usually able to work through any psychological problems with the help of self-analysis. If Mercury or Pluto receives square aspects from the Moon, Saturn, or any personal planet, these subjects can sometimes seem reluctant to relinquish their problems, but if aspects from these planets are positive, they should be able to talk them through freely with friends, once they have reached their own conclusions about them.

Positive aspects   If there is a trine or sextile between Mercury and Pluto, the subject will display a talent for detail and for exploring every topic in depth. If Mercury or Pluto is a personal planet, the individual will feel a need to explore and analyse the self, just as with the conjunction, but the result may be rather more easily achieved.

Gemini Star Map
This 18th-century star map shows the symbol for Gemini. The Twins signify the duality of the sign.

Negative aspects   Secretiveness is common, and these individuals often find it difficult to discuss personal problems. Obsessive tendencies and stubbornness are present if fixed signs are involved. If evidence of nervous tension is shown elsewhere in the horoscope, negative aspects between Mercury and Pluto can have an adverse effect on the health, causing constipation, stomach upsets, or ulcers, especially if the person is prone to worry. Relaxation exercises will be helpful.

MERCURY'S ASPECTS TO
THE ASCENDANT

Conjunction   Mercury will add lively, bright, intelligent qualities to individuals when it is conjunct the Ascendant in their birth chart. They are quick-thinking and versatile but often restless. They often need to communicate their feelings and thoughts, and are very talkative. Their nervous systems can be highly sensitive but work well provided that Mercury is positively aspected by other planets. If Mercury receives negative aspects, there could be some nervous strain and tension. If Mercury is in the twelfth house, the subject may be secretive, although the imagination and intuition are likely to be heightened.

Positive aspects   A trine or square between Mercury and the Ascendant will help to integrate the personality and bring characteristics similar to those of the conjunction, such as liveliness and versatility, but unless Mercury falls in the Sun sign its effect will not be as powerful. It is important to consider the house position of Mercury, because the area of life that the house represents is likely to benefit more strongly than usual from Mercury's qualities.

Negative aspects   Between Mercury and the Ascendant, negative aspects cause tension and nervousness in the subject, and he or she will be inclined to talk too much when agitated. There may be a tendency towards hypochondria, and this will be accentuated if anxiety is indicated elsewhere in the chart.

MERCURY'S ASPECTS TO
THE MIDHEAVEN

Conjunction   The individual will need and enjoy many career changes. There will be a flair for work in communications and the media. Teaching and the travel industry may appeal, but the need for variety should be expressed within the confines of a carefully chosen career, otherwise there will be a tendency to move around so much that real progress is inhibited.

Positive aspects   These will have a similar effect as the conjunction but are less powerful. There is an added emphasis on the positive Mercury areas, and subjects will be more able to avoid restlessness in their career and keep their objectives constant.

Negative aspects   These individuals experience above-average nervous strain and are plagued by worry when there are problems at work or if decisions need to be made about their direction in life. This will be emphasized if Mercury is a personal planet. Look to other areas of the chart to see how the subject can combat this influence.

THE ASPECTS OF VENUS

The position of Venus in a birth chart, the sign it occupies, and the house it rules will reveal how the subject relates to others, and in what area of life he or she desires companionship. Venus also indicates problems that a person might experience in relationships and social friendships, as well as aesthetic tastes and material desires. When Venus is aspected to other planets, it can add harmony and refinement to them. Aspects help to reveal the subject's ability to attract others, and also the way in which material success can be gained. Venus is beneficent, therefore negative aspects are generally harmless.

For Venus' aspects to the Sun
see the Sun's aspects to Venus,
page 77.
For Venus' aspects to the Moon
see page 81.
For Venus' aspects to Mercury
see Mercury's aspects to Venus,
page 82.

VENUS' ASPECTS TO
MARS

Conjunction A conjunction formed between Venus and Mars accentuates and emphasizes the love and sex life, in a splendidly mutual way. Venus refines the coarseness of Mars, and Mars adds spice to gentle Venus. Exuberance, sexual appetite, and enthusiasm are all intensified, and the individual will be very attentive to the needs of a lover. The attitude to love and sex will be very much in the manner of the sign in which the conjunction falls – passionate in a fire sign, romantic in a water sign, intellectual in an air sign, and sensual in an earth sign. These characteristics will be amplified if the Sun falls in the same sign.

Positive aspects Trines and sextiles work in a similar manner to a conjunction, and confer a happy and energetic attitude towards love and relationships. Subjects are likely to have a successful and fulfilling marriage, because they are prepared to make sure their partner is satisfied. They are also likely to be socially inclined and popular with friends and colleagues. This popularity can sometimes aid them financially.

The Bull
Taurus, symbolized by the Bull, is ruled by Venus. The planet also rules Libra.

Negative aspects Passion will be increased, and the attitude to love enlivened, but there can be tension, and some effort must be made to relax and enjoy sex. In some cases, emotional problems are suppressed, especially if the Moon also receives any negative aspects from Saturn, Uranus, or Pluto. The individual may be a victim of unkindness and might need to develop a thick skin. These problems tend to be more difficult to cope with if Venus dominates the chart, but somewhat easier if Mars is the stronger planet.

VENUS' ASPECTS TO
JUPITER

Conjunction At its best, this conjunction gives the individual an idealistic and philosophical outlook, contributing generosity and charm, which will make him or her popular and affectionate. Sometimes there is a tendency to be sybaritic, and a preponderance of trine and sextile aspects elsewhere in the chart can make a person rather too charming, and likely to trade on the fact. If literary creativity is suggested elsewhere in the horoscope, the conjunction will support this.

Positive aspects Trines and sextiles between Venus and Jupiter are useful for anyone dealing with the public, for they contribute charm of manner and the ability to please. They also increase the probability of these individuals living to a ripe old age and the likelihood that they will experience few financial problems.

Negative aspects Both Venus and Jupiter are traditionally held to be "beneficial" planets, so negative aspects between them cause little trouble – although restlessness and discontent can sometimes put in brief appearances. Recklessness in investment can also show itself, as may over-indulgence in food and drink, leading to weight gain.

VENUS' ASPECTS TO
SATURN

Conjunction Shyness can often be the result of this influence, and the affections will be inhibited; personal relationships are sometimes difficult to sustain, and in the love life there may be disappointments. These people can be very cautious about commiting themselves because emotional security is important to them. The choice of an older partner may be the result of this tendency. Occasionally, devotion and duty directed towards parents can result in the postponement of the individual's own emotional life.

PLANETS	
☉	SUN
☽	MOON
☿	MERCURY
♀	VENUS
♂	MARS
♃	JUPITER
♄	SATURN
♅	URANUS
♆	NEPTUNE
♇	PLUTO

SIGNS	
♈	ARIES
♉	TAURUS
♊	GEMINI
♋	CANCER
♌	LEO
♍	VIRGO
♎	LIBRA
♏	SCORPIO
♐	SAGITTARIUS
♑	CAPRICORN
♒	AQUARIUS
♓	PISCES

Positive aspects These are less difficult than the conjunction but often contribute financial hardship. This is because whatever is desired (Venus) is often frustrated (Saturn). If Venus occupies a luxury-loving sign such as Taurus, Leo, or Libra, this effect will be felt even more strongly. These aspects can make individuals very inhibited, but once they feel emotionally secure they will be completely faithful.

Negative aspects These can be even more constricting than the conjunction, but if the Sun or Moon makes a positive aspect to Pluto, or Pluto makes one to the Ascendant, inhibition could be very successfully treated by therapy. If enthusiasm and emotional energy are indicated elsewhere in the birth chart, the inhibition will be less overwhelming.

VENUS' ASPECTS TO
URANUS

Conjunction Although people with this aspect in their birth chart have considerable personal magnetism and sex appeal, they will hesitate to commit themselves to an emotional relationship and they are likely to maintain a cool distance from their partner. They possess a high level of rather agitated emotional tension that will need positive expression, perhaps creatively, or through some unusual and original interest. There is usually an element of perversity and self-will in the personality of these individuals. If foolhardiness or impetuousness is indicated elsewhere in the horoscope – look to see if Mars is in a fire sign – then this conjunction will exacerbate it.

Positive aspects Trines and sextiles are very similar in their effect to the conjunction but less forceful. They encourage originality and sometimes creativity, but perversity and even eccentricity are likely to arise, too. These aspects cool the emotions, and subjects will prefer to keep their distance from others, even those people they profess to love.

Negative aspects These individuals usually show considerable strain and tension, which will be expressed in their attitude towards relationships. It is often almost impossible for them to relax, and they can be difficult and highly contrary, single-mindedly pursuing their own intentions at the expense of any other considerations. Relaxation techniques such as yoga will help the subject combat stress.

VENUS' ASPECTS TO
NEPTUNE

Conjunction These people tend to be romantic, idealistic, and over-sensitive, and this too often leads to disappointment in love. This is most likely to be the case if the conjunction falls in Libra. These people have a strong appreciation of beauty in art and in nature, and they are likely to possess good taste. If the conjunction is in Sagittarius, there will be a particular fondness for animals. A conjunction between Venus and Neptune can weaken the will to some degree, and when these individuals have a particular liking for something that might be bad for them, such as rich food or alcohol, they find it difficult to give it up.

Positive aspects If these subjects' charts show them to be down-to-earth, practical, and materialistic, trines or sextiles between Venus and Neptune have a softening effect on their personalities and give them additional sympathy and kindness. They sometimes attempt to conceal their compassionate side for fear of appearing weak and gullible. Artistic ability is likely to be increased by these aspects, and if musical talent is suggested elsewhere in the birth chart the individuals may even make their living by playing a musical instrument. They are often accused of daydreaming and are sometimes subject to visionary experiences.

Negative aspects Restlessness will certainly be a problem, especially if it is also indicated elsewhere in the birth chart, and people with these aspects may always be discontented. Venus brings a desire for comfort and material success, but Neptune can make these desires unfocused and hard to attain. If the Sun and Moon are also negatively aspected to each other, there can be serious problems. The subject may drift from job to job and house to house, always looking for contentment but never quite finding it. The sensitivity contributed by the conjunction is increased with negative aspects, and these people are likely to have an idealistic attitude towards love. If Neptune is in Scorpio, they tend to be overwhelmed by their emotions.

The Seer
Astrologers were once consulted about every life event, including the outcome of war.

Sidebar (left margin):

PLANETS

SUN

MOON

MERCURY

VENUS

MARS

JUPITER

SATURN

URANUS

NEPTUNE

PLUTO

SIGNS

ARIES

TAURUS

GEMINI

CANCER

LEO

VIRGO

LIBRA

SCORPIO

SAGITTARIUS

CAPRICORN

AQUARIUS

PISCES

VENUS' ASPECTS TO
PLUTO

Conjunction The need for fulfilment in a loving sexual relationship is very strong indeed. Someone with this aspect tends to fall in love deeply and passionately, and will need that love to be reciprocated in an equally powerful way. If the conjunction is aspected by Saturn, or if Uranus joins the conjunction of Venus and Pluto (in which case all three planets are likely to be in Virgo) the subject may find that therapy is needed to clear the psychological blockages that restrict sensual gratification. Both Venus and Pluto influence finance, and this powerful conjunction sometimes gives a flair for investment and a financial ability that could be successfully employed in a career involved with money, such as accountancy.

Positive aspects The emotional level is high, and it is essential that emotions are expressed in a fulfilling way. In addition, there are strong powers of attraction and often a seductive demeanour that will be accentuated if Venus is in Scorpio.

Negative aspects Intensity and passion are sometimes blocked by these negative aspects, and they can prevent a positive flow of emotion. These people do not find it easy to talk through problems with friends, especially if there are indications of anxiety or inhibition elsewhere in the horoscope. Counselling by a professional may be helpful.

VENUS' ASPECTS TO
THE ASCENDANT

Conjunction With Venus in the first house, the characteristics of the Ascendant will be enhanced. These individuals will be loving and affectionate, and will need a

An Allegory of Astrology
In this 17th-century allegorical painting, astrology is portrayed as a woman studying herself.

harmonious and peaceful life, which they will be adept at creating, and through which they will sail with a somewhat lethargic, languid manner. It is also important for them to have a contented emotional relationship and a sound financial base – a lack of either of these will be extremely disconcerting. Should Venus be afflicted by negative aspects from Mars, Saturn, Uranus, or Pluto, there could be health problems and headaches. A negative aspect from Neptune suggests over-indulgence in food and drink, which could cause weight gain or urinary difficulties. If Venus is in the twelfth house, there can be reclusive or escapist tendencies. Read Venus in the Twelfth House on page 61 for an interpretation of this position, noting that the influence is enhanced because Venus conjuncts the Ascendant.

Positive aspects These individuals will be warm and affectionate, and they need to give and receive love from an equally sympathetic person. They will enjoy a busy and rewarding social life, and gain satisfaction from giving other people pleasure. They have a strong aesthetic sense and like to surround themselves with beautiful objects.

Negative aspects Squares and oppositions between Venus and the Ascendant encourage the subject to be self-indulgent. Resentfulness and indecisiveness can be problems. If an opposition falls with Venus in the seventh house, too much will be expected of partners, and there will be a tendency to try to buy love with over-generous gifts. If Venus is in the sixth house, health problems may arise due to a lack of exercise or over-eating.

VENUS' ASPECTS TO
THE MIDHEAVEN

Conjunction This aspect signifies a considerate colleague who is always ready to listen sympathetically to others' difficulties or queries, and take account of their suggestions. At work, however, these people tend to find routine somewhat difficult, and to procrastinate and become distracted. In emotional partnerships, they are sympathetic and caring.

Positive aspects Pleasant working conditions are important, and the work itself needs to be enjoyable and satisfying. If it is dull, a good rapport with colleagues will rescue these people from boredom. These aspects indicate that the relationship with the parents will be good.

Negative aspects Oppositions and squares between Venus and the Midheaven can suggest uncongenial working conditions. The subject has a tendency to over-react to situations at work, and discontent results from getting things out of perspective.

PLANETS

SUN

MOON

MERCURY

♀
VENUS

MARS

JUPITER

SATURN

URANUS

NEPTUNE

PLUTO

SIGNS

♈
ARIES

♉
TAURUS

♊
GEMINI

♋
CANCER

♌
LEO

♍
VIRGO

♎
LIBRA

♏
SCORPIO

♐
SAGITTARIUS

♑
CAPRICORN

♒
AQUARIUS

♓
PISCES

PLANETS

SUN

MOON

MERCURY

VENUS

♂
MARS

JUPITER

SATURN

URANUS

NEPTUNE

PLUTO

SIGNS

♈
ARIES

♉
TAURUS

♊
GEMINI

♋
CANCER

♌
LEO

♍
VIRGO

♎
LIBRA

♏
SCORPIO

♐
SAGITTARIUS

♑
CAPRICORN

♒
AQUARIUS

♓
PISCES

THE ASPECTS OF MARS

Mars invigorates and energizes an individual physically, emotionally, and intellectually, and its sign and house position in the birth chart reveal the subject's ability for dynamic action. If Mars is positively aspected, its powerful energies are likely to be directed in a constructive manner. Favourable aspects from Saturn will bring discipline; from Mercury, intelligence; and from Jupiter, altruism. If Mars is afflicted, however, these energies can cause aggression, rash action, and outbursts of temper. In this case, it is vital to discover ways in which the subject can control and channel the energy rewardingly.

For Mars' aspects to the Sun see the Sun's aspects to Mars, page 77.
For Mars' aspects to the Moon see page 81.
For Mars' aspects to Mercury see Mercury's aspects to Mars, page 82.
For Mars' aspects to Venus see Venus' aspects to Mars, page 85.

The Headstrong Ram
The Arien Ram personifies the dynamic energy that is bestowed by Aries' ruling planet, Mars.

MARS' ASPECTS TO
JUPITER

Conjunction These are plain-speaking people who know where they are going and are determined to get there. Forthright, decisive initiative is shown, and a great deal of enterprise. They will achieve objectives that seem over-ambitious to less determined people. They are daring investors with considerable financial acumen but should heed the advice of others, especially if the conjunction falls in Aries or Sagittarius, when risk-taking may be a real problem. These people are combative and unafraid of disputing with colleagues or employers.

Positive aspects These aspects contribute many of the attributes of the conjunction but rather less forcibly. The subjects are able to keep their enthusiasm under control and find it easy to persuade others to accept their innovative ideas. They have lively minds in active bodies, and both intellectual and sporting activities will benefit, particularly if either planet is personalized.

Negative aspects Intellectual and physical energy will be enhanced and exaggerated. An inability to be temperate about anything is difficult for these people, and the health can be undermined by immoderation. Positive aspects from the Sun or Saturn will control this influence.

MARS' ASPECTS TO
SATURN

Conjunction This very potent influence works unevenly, giving energy and determination one day, and gloom and inertia the next. Self-will and obstinacy can also present themselves, and there may be a tendency to be accident-prone, perhaps because of carelessness. Exercise is recommended to keep arthritis and rheumatism at bay.

Positive aspects Great powers of endurance will ensure that these individuals can work in difficult conditions. They have a strong will to succeed but need to find a focus for their abundant energy.

Negative aspects Life is earnest for those with negative aspects between Mars and Saturn. The cold winds of reality soon begin to blow on any enthusiasm. Energy is ruthlessly expended with exhausting results, and this needs to be controlled if there is not to be damage to the constitution. A steady exercise regime will be particularly helpful.

MARS' ASPECTS TO
URANUS

Conjunction Great determination and obstinate self-will are caused by this conjunction. Stubbornness and intolerance will be characteristics if the aspect falls in a fixed sign, and in any event the individual will be frank and outspoken. If the aspect falls in the tenth house, or either or both planets are conjunct the Midheaven, the individual will find it easier to understand that he or she should not take advantage of the possession of power.

Positive aspects Trines and sextiles between Mars and Uranus offer a high degree of nervous energy, which the individual will be able to use in a controlled and focused way. These people tend to be independent and have intellectual originality, as well as a flair for technology, science, and engineering. Quick responses will be made in any emergency.

Negative aspects These rather undesirable aspects denote a strong degree of self-will, perversity, and excessive argumentativeness.

These people need to be aware of how much pain can be inflicted on others by uncontrolled selfishness. They will possess a great desire to win, which will often bring success but at the cost of mental stress.

MARS' ASPECTS TO NEPTUNE

Conjunction Someone with Mars conjunct Neptune is likely to have a rich fantasy life, and sexual passion will be sensually expressed. Physical energy is often depleted, however, leaving the individual restless and discontent, often without knowing why. A creative interest of some sort may ease the situation – but dependence on so-called recreational drugs must be discouraged.

Positive aspects These aspects encourage creativity and originality, and a rich imagination will need to be expressed through some form of creative art. The emotions are also heightened, and sexual pleasure is increased. These people are sensitive and intense lovers, but when they fall in love they will need to keep at least one foot on the ground.

Negative aspects Escapism is a danger for these individuals, who have a tendency to turn to drugs – cigarettes, alcohol, or even more dangerous substances – when they are under stress. If either Neptune or Mars is in a water sign, moodiness may also be a problem. Look for other elements in the chart that will help the subject to combat these weaknesses, such as the Sun, Moon, or Ascendant in an earth sign.

MARS' ASPECTS TO PLUTO

Conjunction If well aspected by the Sun or Moon, this conjunction contributes a very powerful driving force and much determination to somewhat stubborn individuals. However, negative aspects to the conjunction cause them to suffer from pent-up energy that will

Look to the Skies
Turkish astronomers used sophisticated equipment to study the stars and planets.

be released with difficulty. They are likely to benefit from learning a sport such as karate or judo, where the energy can be expressed in a controlled manner. These people's tempers are easily aroused, and if the conjunction is in Scorpio or is joined by Uranus in Virgo, they can have a cruel streak in their nature.

Positive aspects A high level of physical and emotional energy can turn these people into workaholics. From time to time, they will find themselves compelled to make sweeping changes to their lives.

Negative aspects As with the other aspects between these two planets, emotional and physical energy is increased. The tendency to work until breaking point is exacerbated, and the attainment of objectives can become an obsession. Obstacles seem to expand as they are tackled, and satisfaction may be elusive.

MARS' ASPECTS TO THE ASCENDANT

Conjunction If Mars is in the first house, reread page 62, as the characteristics of that position will be strongly emphasized. If it is in the twelfth house, reread Mars in the

twelfth house, on page 63. If Mars is in the first house, physical energy will be increased; if it is in the twelfth house, emotional energy will be strengthened. An inclination to be selfish will be greater if Mars is in the first than if it is in the twelfth house, but if the latter is the case the individual may be over-secretive.

Positive aspects These increase the physical energy, and an involvement in sports or a physically demanding job is advisable to expend the energy positively. The individual is likely to possess a strong independent streak and an ever-present need for action.

Negative aspects There will be a tendency to overwork, which may lower the vitality, especially if Mars is in the sixth house. If it is in the seventh house, a lively sexual relationship is necessary, but this placing also brings a tendency to quarrel. It is important with any aspect to Mars to take the house and sign placing into consideration, because this will reveal which aspect of the subject's life will be affected.

MARS' ASPECTS TO THE MIDHEAVEN

Conjunction The will to succeed is paramount, and the individual will have a great deal of ambition and independence. These people need either to be emotionally involved in their careers or to have a compelling interest into which they can channel their energy. They are also highly competitive and need to be in a prominent position in their social lives as well as in their careers.

Positive aspects There will be the same focused energy as with the conjunction. Enthusiasm for work will be infectious, and colleagues will be supported and encouraged.

Negative aspects These subjects work hard, sometimes to breaking point, but tend to argue with colleagues. Patience towards people with slower minds needs to be cultivated.

PLANETS

SUN

MOON

MERCURY

VENUS

MARS

JUPITER

SATURN

URANUS

NEPTUNE

PLUTO

SIGNS

ARIES

TAURUS

GEMINI

CANCER

LEO

VIRGO

LIBRA

SCORPIO

SAGITTARIUS

CAPRICORN

AQUARIUS

PISCES

PLANETS

SUN

MOON

MERCURY

VENUS

MARS

♃
JUPITER

SATURN

URANUS

NEPTUNE

PLUTO

SIGNS

ARIES

TAURUS

GEMINI

CANCER

LEO

VIRGO

LIBRA

SCORPIO

SAGITTARIUS

CAPRICORN

AQUARIUS

PISCES

THE ASPECTS OF JUPITER

Jupiter is associated primarily with expansion – with learning, philosophy, and languages. It also encourages optimism and extravagance, and its sign and house position in a birth chart reveal how subjects expand their mental capacity and how they relate to others in social situations. A well-aspected Jupiter will enhance an individual's personality, but if the planet is afflicted the subject may lack moderation and be over-ambitious. When interpreting Jupiter's aspects to the outer planets, the houses and signs involved reveal what area of life is affected. If the planets are personalized, these aspects will have a stronger effect on the subject.

For Jupiter's aspects to the Sun
see the Sun's aspects to Jupiter, page 77.
For Jupiter's aspects to the Moon
see page 81.
For Jupiter's aspects to Mercury
see Mercury's aspects to Jupiter, page 82.
For Jupiter's aspects to Venus
see Venus' aspects to Jupiter, page 85.
For Jupiter's aspects to Mars
see Mars' aspects to Jupiter, page 88.

The Meaning of Life
Throughout the ages, people have looked to the stars for answers to questions about life.

JUPITER'S ASPECTS TO SATURN

Conjunction   The two giants of the solar system combine to produce optimism and common sense when they are conjunct in a person's chart. There should be a balanced outlook on life, and enthusiasm will be controlled and used in a positive manner. Of the two planets, Saturn usually has the stronger influence, bestowing a somewhat dour effect on the individual and causing him or her to feel gloomy and depressed without reason. However, Saturn also contributes a sense of purpose, staying power, and a very practical approach to solving problems. Sometimes there is conflict between the expansion of Jupiter and the contraction of Saturn. The person will have to overcome obstacles in order to achieve goals, and projects started with enthusiasm sometimes end in difficulty. If either planet is personalized, its effect on the individual will be much stronger.

Positive aspects   Trines and sextiles between Saturn and Jupiter denote an individual who has a balanced outlook on life. The common sense and practicality of Saturn blend well with the extroverted enthusiasm and optimism of Jupiter, producing breadth of vision combined with caution. These people should listen to their inner voice because the advice tends to be reliable. They are adept at making plans for the future and carrying out such plans. Their judgement will be sound, and they will work out problems coherently.

Negative aspects   Individuals who have negative aspects between Jupiter and Saturn often feel that they have failed to achieve their potential. Inner discontent, or a lack of self-confidence, is often at the root of their problems, and they tend to see themselves as failures even when they are successful. Look at the rest of the birth chart to see if this can be combated. For instance, a well-aspected Mars will help.

JUPITER'S ASPECTS TO URANUS

Conjunction   Individuals with Jupiter conjunct Uranus in their birth chart will have highly original minds, and be forward-looking, humanitarian, and benevolent. Their sense of humour tends to be off-beat and charming, and will give them a positive and cheerful outlook on life. If the conjunction is negatively aspected, tension and restlessness may arise but will not usually present insurmountable problems.

Positive aspects   The qualities of the conjunction will be seen, and if extroversion is shown elsewhere in the chart – for instance, if the Sun is in a fire sign – the individual will be extremely popular. There will be a strong element of determination, but also a degree of eccentricity that, as long as it is controlled, will do no harm. Positive aspects between Jupiter and Uranus will help the subject to develop his or her potential.

Negative aspects   Subjects who have squares or oppositions between Jupiter and Uranus will have a restless and eccentric personality; this is particularly so if either planet is personalized. Fleeting enthusiasms will be embraced and then quickly rejected, often after money has been spent on them. Independence can be carried to extremes – for instance, help is likely to be rejected even when it is needed. Pomposity and stubbornness may be a problem if Jupiter or Uranus is personalized.

JUPITER'S ASPECTS TO
NEPTUNE

Conjunction   Jupiter ruled Pisces before Neptune, so there exists a considerable affinity between these two planets. This conjunction offers idealism, humility, and optimism, as well as a subtly expressed caring instinct. Spirituality is often present, although not necessarily linked to a conventional religion. The fantasy life is rich, and if there are few signs of practicality in the birth chart, subjects will have a tendency to daydream, sometimes to the extent that they accomplish little in life. If any of a subject's personal planets are in earth signs, or if Mars is well aspected, he or she should be able to control this problem.

Positive aspects   These are similar to the conjunction in effect, but are not as strong and can easily be swamped by more robust elements in the birth chart. If subjects have their Sun, Moon, or Ascendant in Pisces or Sagittarius, they will be highly sensitive. If not, the subtle, gentle qualities of these aspects will add delicacy and sympathy even to the strongest of birth charts.

Negative aspects   As with the conjunction and positive aspects, kindness, sympathy, and sensitivity to suffering are bestowed – but the individual can be absent-minded and dreamy to the point of inefficiency. The emotional level is increased, and the imagination is colourful but not always positively expressed – there can be a tendency towards self-deception or dishonesty.

JUPITER'S ASPECTS TO
PLUTO

Conjunction   If this aspect falls in the tenth house, or either planet also forms a conjunction with the Midheaven, there will be an almost overwhelming desire for power. Wherever the conjunction falls, the need of these people to make material progress is very strong, with a near-obsessive enthusiasm to attain objectives. This strong sense of purpose can be advantageous provided it is kept under control, but if not, the subject is likely to be ruthless. Together with personal magnetism and leadership qualities, there are the foundations here for a dictator – whether in government, the office, or the home.

Positive aspects   Many of the qualities of the conjunction are present, but there will be an added intelligence that not only helps these subjects to achieve their goals but also enables them to control any excessive desires for power.

Negative aspects   As with the other aspects of these two planets, power of leadership is combined with the stern pursuit of objectives. If Uranus conjuncts Pluto in Virgo (as it did between 1963 and 1969) and Jupiter negatively aspects both planets, there will be a tendency to mislead and deceive others. Subjects should be encouraged to develop any sensitive qualities bestowed by their Sun, Moon, or Ascendant.

JUPITER'S ASPECTS TO
THE ASCENDANT

Conjunction   If Jupiter is in the first house, the subject will be open-minded and highly optimistic with an excellent intellect. He or she will be fun-loving but also have a philosophical bent and a strong sense of justice. If Jupiter is in the twelfth house, the person will be less extroverted, and the reflective side of the planet will have its effect. There may be a strong sense of vocation.

The Archer
Sagittarius, symbolized by the Archer, is ruled by Jupiter. Until Neptune was discovered in 1846, Jupiter also ruled Pisces.

Positive aspects   A trine or sextile between Jupiter and the Ascendant will have an effect similar to that of the conjunction in the first house but less powerful. The subject will be positive, popular with others, and likely to find happiness in love.

Negative aspects   These individuals tend to exaggerate and show off, which alienates others and causes problems in both their personal and professional lives. If they can recognize their problem, they should be able to stifle these traits.

JUPITER'S ASPECTS TO
THE MIDHEAVEN

Conjunction   These individuals have great potential for success and are usually contented. They are active, with an optimistic outlook on life, and have enthusiasm for everything they undertake, although they lack the ability to concentrate on details.

Positive aspects   Optimistic and enthusiastic, these people will take calculated risks in order to achieve their objectives. Their self-confidence increases with success, and they are proud of their achievements.

Negative aspects   Subjects tend to show off and enjoy ostentatious and grand gestures. They are usually successful – but may not be as popular as they think.

PLANETS

SUN

MOON

MERCURY

VENUS

MARS

JUPITER

SATURN

URANUS

NEPTUNE

PLUTO

SIGNS

ARIES

TAURUS

GEMINI

CANCER

LEO

VIRGO

LIBRA

SCORPIO

SAGITTARIUS

CAPRICORN

AQUARIUS

PISCES

PLANETS

SUN

MOON

MERCURY

VENUS

MARS

JUPITER

SATURN

URANUS

NEPTUNE

PLUTO

SIGNS

ARIES

TAURUS

GEMINI

CANCER

LEO

VIRGO

LIBRA

SCORPIO

SAGITTARIUS

CAPRICORN

AQUARIUS

PISCES

THE ASPECTS OF SATURN

Saturn represents authority, discipline, and inhibition. The planet teaches us how to overcome difficulties by learning from experience. A strong Saturn in the chart indicates ambition and motivation. This drive and determination to succeed will manifest itself in the areas ruled by the planets Saturn aspects.

Below we deal with the aspects Saturn makes to the planets positioned beyond it in the solar system: Uranus, Neptune, and Pluto. These planets appear in a similar position in the charts of a great many people. However, by aspecting other planets, their influence is powerful and should not be underestimated.

For Saturn's aspects to the Sun see the Sun's aspects to Saturn, page 78.

For Saturn's aspects to the Moon see page 81.

For Saturn's aspects to Mercury see Mercury's aspects to Saturn, page 83.

For Saturn's aspects to Venus see Venus' aspects to Saturn, page 85.

For Saturn's aspects to Mars see Mars' aspects to Saturn, page 88.

For Saturn's aspects to Jupiter see Jupiter's aspects to Saturn, page 90.

SATURN'S ASPECTS TO URANUS

Conjunction This powerful and energetic aspect most recently occurred in Taurus in the 1940s, and in Sagittarius and Capricorn in 1986–89. Conjunctions of Saturn tend to indicate hard work and a drive to succeed, and from Sagittarius this conjunction produces a broad and original mind combined with an industrious and self-disciplined character. When the conjunction crosses the signs (with Saturn in Capricorn and Uranus in Sagittarius) Saturn's influence tends to dominate, because the planet rules Capricorn. As a result, the individual will adopt a more cautious and conservative approach to life. When both planets occupy Taurus or Capricorn, the outlook tends to be extremely sober, staid, and conventional. If Scorpio is emphasized by a personal planet,

The Reaper
Saturn was an agricultural god, and was particularly associated with harvest time.

ambition and aspiration may develop into a hunger for power. When Saturn and Uranus aspect the Sun, Moon, Ascendant, or Midheaven, a charismatic and inspiring personality will win many friends and admirers.

Positive aspects Whether they are conservative or unconventional, these people are very tolerant of the beliefs of others. Their originality and imagination is tempered by an innate sense of caution, and they will adopt a lively yet practical approach to life.

Negative aspects The pessimism of Saturn and the tension of Uranus may be exacerbated if these elements appear elsewhere in the chart. As a result, those in a position of power may appear very severe, cold, and unapproachable. If the planets are

personalized, the individual will benefit from relaxation techniques such as yoga.

SATURN'S ASPECTS TO NEPTUNE

Conjunction This conjunction occurs approximately every thirty-six years. It occupied Leo in 1917 and Libra in the 1950s, and appears in the majority of birth charts of those people born between March 1988 and November 1990. During this most recent period, a double conjunction occurred. When Uranus was travelling through the last degrees of Sagittarius and into Capricorn, the planet was briefly conjunct with both Saturn and Neptune. Consequently, everything that is discussed above regarding the conjunction of Saturn and Uranus will also apply here. In addition, Neptune will contribute a gentle, dreamy, and nebulous atmosphere to the ambitious and determined influence of Saturn and Neptune. The discipline of Saturn will enable people to use the inspiration and compassion of Neptune in a practical manner. All three planets occupy earth signs, and the humanitarian instincts of Uranus, combined with the great sensitivity and idealism of Neptune, may have brought about the green movement and strengthened concerns about protecting the Earth.

Positive aspects Kindness and sympathy come naturally to people with these aspects, and they are always ready to lend a helping hand

and a sympathetic ear. Due to the motivation of Saturn combined with the idealism of Neptune, they will live up to their high ideals. Saturn will also curb the more fanciful and self-indulgent side of Neptune. These subjects may display scientific ability, and are drawn to chemistry and scientific research.

Negative aspects If Saturn or Neptune is personalized, these aspects can encourage impracticality and confused thinking. The limiting influence of Saturn may restrict the flow of emotion, and any creative potential can be thwarted by a lack of confidence and self-esteem.

SATURN'S ASPECTS TO
PLUTO

Conjunction This conjunction occurred in Leo during the late 1940s and again in Libra in the early 1980s. This aspect will cause Saturn's need for status to combine with Pluto's powerful urges, resulting in strong ambitions and aspirations. These people will try to channel their abundant energies into achieving their objectives. If the two planets form a conjunction to the Sun, Moon, or Ascendant, the individuals may suffer from stress and tension, which will be manifested in the form of physical ailments. If the planets are personalized, the effect of this conjunction is likely to be stronger.

Positive aspects These will offer increased determination and energy to the subject. Stubbornness may sometimes be evident if the planets are personalized. Positive aspects will enable individuals to overcome anxiety and worry by adopting a cheerful and optimistic attitude.

Negative aspects There may be some obsessive behaviour patterns, which may be difficult to resolve. These people tend to bury their heads in the sand rather than face up to difficulties. However, few problems should arise – unless the planets are personalized.

SATURN'S ASPECTS TO
THE ASCENDANT

Conjunction Usually this aspect produces a reliable and responsible personality, and a serious, sensible outlook on life. However, with this aspect, the house position of Saturn is also particularly relevant. From the first house, the conjunction is likely to cause shyness and a lack of self-confidence, especially in the young. These people should be able to overcome their insecurities, due to their abundance of common sense. However, if Saturn receives negative aspects from the Sun or Moon, they will find it difficult to boost their confidence, and depression is possible, especially if the Moon aspects Saturn.

Positive aspects These contribute common sense, caution, and strong practicality, and will be helpful to those with a great deal of air or fire in their horoscope, since they will act as a safety valve to steady and control emotion.

Negative aspects These may inhibit the positive and optimistic areas of the personality. A rather gloomy and pessimistic outlook, together with slightly low vitality, will be the result, and complaints will be common. However, these aspects may be overcome by the strength of the Sun or Ascendant signs.

SATURN'S ASPECTS TO
THE MIDHEAVEN

Conjunction Saturn will be a very important planet in this context, tending to load individuals with responsibility while encouraging them to do well. Events over which they have no control often project these subjects into the limelight. They have a tendency to distance themselves from others, and their aspirations are so powerful that often they do not have time for fun and relaxation. Consequently, these people may begrudge periods spent with their partners and children.

Positive aspects These people possess all the positive Saturnine qualities: practicality, common sense, and discipline. They will be ambitious and determined, and these aspects will help them reach the top.

Negative aspects There may be setbacks, and attempts to progress will sometimes be frustrated, so goals will be achieved slowly but surely. These people may lack self-confidence, and as a result may be rather too cautious and shy away from challenges. A well-placed Mars or Jupiter may counter the effect.

Capricorn the Goat
Saturn originally ruled Capricorn and Aquarius but now rules only Capricorn.

PLANETS

SUN

MOON

MERCURY

VENUS

MARS

JUPITER

SATURN

URANUS

NEPTUNE

PLUTO

SIGNS

ARIES

TAURUS

GEMINI

CANCER

LEO

VIRGO

LIBRA

SCORPIO

SAGITTARIUS

CAPRICORN

AQUARIUS

PISCES

THE ASPECTS OF URANUS, NEPTUNE, AND PLUTO

The aspects that the three "modern" planets, Uranus, Neptune, and Pluto, form to one another stay within orb for long periods. Therefore, they will be in the charts of everyone born during a certain time and should be regarded as having a generational effect. However, when these distant planets make an aspect to the Ascendant or Midheaven, or a personal planet in a birth chart, their influence is likely to have a powerful effect on the subject.

-URANUS-

For Uranus' aspects to the Sun see the Sun's aspects to Uranus, page 78.
For Uranus' aspects to the Moon, see page 81.
For Uranus' aspects to Mercury see Mercury's aspects to Uranus, page 83.
For Uranus' aspects to Venus see Venus' aspects to Uranus, page 86.
For Uranus' aspects to Mars see Mars' aspects to Uranus, page 88.
For Uranus' aspects to Jupiter see Jupiter's aspects to Uranus, page 90.
For Uranus' aspects to Saturn see Saturn's aspects to Uranus, page 92.

URANUS' ASPECTS TO
NEPTUNE

Conjunction This conjunction, which occurs approximately every 171 years, appears in the charts of people born between January 1989 and February 1998. Uranus' humanitarianism and the spiritual influence of Neptune, combined in the practical sign of Capricorn, suggest these people will be very concerned with the environment.

Positive aspects Originality blends with imagination when Uranus and Neptune are positively aspected. This is an excellent influence for those engaged in scientific research, where intuition is guided by logical thought.

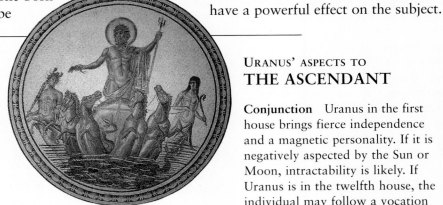

The Lord of the Seas
Seahorses drew Neptune's chariot when he rose from his palace in the depths.

Negative aspects Confusion and tension, if indicated elsewhere in the birth chart, will be exacerbated. Relaxation techniques may help.

URANUS' ASPECTS TO
PLUTO

Conjunction This conjunction last appeared between 1963 and 1969 in Virgo and produced people with enormous vitality who, if they have Virgo personalized or if that sign is on the Midheaven, may lead their generation. If the conjunction is negatively aspected, the individual may have psychological problems.

Positive aspects A tendency to make drastic changes will be a motivating force. Plans are often completed only after considerable effort and difficulty.

Negative aspects The individual tends to be disruptive and will make changes simply for the sake of doing so, usually regretting it later.

URANUS' ASPECTS TO
THE ASCENDANT

Conjunction Uranus in the first house brings fierce independence and a magnetic personality. If it is negatively aspected by the Sun or Moon, intractability is likely. If Uranus is in the twelfth house, the individual may follow a vocation involving considerable sacrifices.

Positive aspects Uranus adds a lively brilliance to the personality and will increase the originality of creative people. Sometimes it bestows dynamic powers of attraction.

Negative aspects These aspects can make a person extremely perverse and unpredictable. A square aspect can be more disruptive and negative than the opposition.

URANUS' ASPECTS TO
THE MIDHEAVEN

Conjunction Drastic changes of direction in the career are likely. These people may be rebellious and like to work independently. There is often originality and even brilliance.

Positive aspects These aspects have an effect similar to that of the conjunction, but the desire for change can adversely affect the course of a career or other goals and ambitions.

Negative aspects These people tend to be over-apprehensive about minor problems and will suffer from stress if pressured by their employer.

-NEPTUNE-

For Neptune's aspects to the Sun see the Sun's aspects to Neptune, page 79.
For Neptune's aspects to the Moon see page 81.
For Neptune's aspects to Mercury see Mercury's aspects to Neptune, page 83.
For Neptune's aspects to Venus see Venus' aspects to Neptune, page 86.
For Neptune's aspects to Mars see Mars' aspects to Neptune, page 89.
For Neptune's aspects to Jupiter see Jupiter's aspects to Neptune, page 91.
For Neptune's aspects to Saturn see Saturn's aspects to Neptune, page 92.
For Neptune's aspects to Uranus see Uranus' aspects to Neptune, page 94.

NEPTUNE'S ASPECTS TO
PLUTO

The sextile Neptune and Pluto move so slowly that the sextile is the only aspect made by the planets in our time. It is not greatly significant but emphasizes intuition and increases the flow of emotion.

NEPTUNE'S ASPECTS TO
THE ASCENDANT

Conjunction In the first house, this aspect saps determination and creates a need for negative escapism. From the twelfth house, the planet bestows altruism, and subjects may carry out good works far from the public eye.

Positive aspects These aspects will soften the rising sign characteristics, and impart intuition and imagination. Creative imagination is likely to be heightened, and these individuals often possess powers of seduction.

Negative aspects Self-deception and a tendency to delude others is likely to accompany a desire to try and escape from reality.

NEPTUNE'S ASPECTS TO
THE MIDHEAVEN

Conjunction The individual will be idealistic and sensitive and, if there are signs of stability and common sense elsewhere in the chart, may use these characteristics in a career.

Positive aspects These influences are helpful if the subject is pursuing a Neptunian career, such as dance, photography, or a caring profession.

Negative aspects Neptune brings a tendency to be devious as well as an underhanded streak. Subjects may curry favour with employers.

-PLUTO-

For Pluto's aspects to the Sun see the Sun's aspects to Pluto, page 79.
For Pluto's aspects to the Moon see page 81.
For Pluto's aspects to Mercury see Mercury's aspects to Pluto, page 84.
For Pluto's aspects to Venus see Venus' aspects to Pluto, page 87.
For Pluto's aspects to Mars see Mars' aspects to Pluto, page 89.
For Pluto's aspects to Jupiter see Jupiter's aspects to Pluto, page 91.
For Pluto's aspects to Saturn see Saturn's aspects to Pluto, page 93.
For Pluto's aspects to Uranus see Uranus' aspects to Pluto, page 94.
For Pluto's aspects to Neptune see Neptune's aspects to Pluto, page 95.

PLUTO'S ASPECTS TO
THE ASCENDANT

Conjunction From the first house, Pluto brings a need to get to the root of every situation and a strong emotional force. From the twelfth house, Pluto will bring a desire for secrecy and a smouldering intensity.

Early Illuminations
Monks, the earliest recorders of European knowledge, reconciled astrological study and religion.

Positive aspects The individual may possess a deep-rooted urge to "move on", constantly making a clean sweep, psychologically as well as physically.

Negative aspects Frustration and the inability to make progress are signalled in those areas of life indicated by Pluto's house position.

PLUTO'S ASPECTS TO
THE MIDHEAVEN

Conjunction This conjunction often suggests that the individual will have a power complex, and he or she will certainly identify with the stronger characteristics of the Midheaven sign. Emotional identification with the career or main objective in life is essential for these people if their energy is to be directed positively.

Positive aspects If Pluto positively aspects the Ascendant, the need for change is psychologically motivated, but when it aspects the Midheaven, change occurs through circumstance. These positive aspects will help the subject to cope with upheaval.

Negative aspects Difficulties and upheavals occur as the result of circumstances that are beyond the individual's control. The Moon's sign and house position will indicate whether these people will have the inner strength to cope.

PLANETS

SUN

MOON

MERCURY

VENUS

MARS

JUPITER

SATURN

URANUS

NEPTUNE

PLUTO

SIGNS

ARIES

TAURUS

GEMINI

CANCER

LEO

VIRGO

LIBRA

SCORPIO

SAGITTARIUS

CAPRICORN

AQUARIUS

PISCES

ACKNOWLEDGMENTS

Key t: *top;* c: *centre;* b: *below;* l: *left;* r: *right.*

ASTROLOGY AND YOU

Photography: Steve Gorton, Colin Keates, Monique Le Luhandre, Harry Taylor.

Artwork: Peter Lawman: pp. 8-19tc. Danuta Mayer: pp. 8-19bc, 23, 24, 27, 28, 31, 32, 35, 36, 39, 40, 43, 44, 47, 48, 49, 50, 51. Jane Thomson: p.82.

Picture Credits: **AKG Photo**: Musee du Louvre 31tc. **Bridgeman Art Library, London**: Private Collection 2tc; Biblioteca Estene, Modena 5tr, 42bl; British Library, London 6, 37bc, 41br, 46bl, 74, 78bl; Château de Versailles 51tc; Derby Museum and Art Gallery 25br; Lauros-Giraudon 33br; Musee Conde, Chantilly 1c, 4c, 22cl; Philip Mould, Historical Portraits Ltd, London 87tl; O'Shea Gallery, London 34bl; Oriental Museum, Durham University 16cb. **British Museum**: 21tr. **Mary Evans Picture Library**: 27tr, 39tl, 47tc, 76c 77tl, 83br, 91br, 93br, 96tc. **Sonia Halliday and Laura Lushington**: 23c, 30bl, 38bl, 43tc, 85c, 88c, 89tc, 94c. **Images Colour Library/Charles Walker Collection**: 3tc, 26bl, 29br, 35c, 45br, 49tl, 52, 55cl, 56br, 58c, 60cl, 62bl, 65tl, 67clb, 69cr, 71br, 73tl, 80c, 81br, 84bl, 86br. **Natural History Museum**: 8tr, 9tr, 10tr, 11tr, 12tr, 13tr, 14tr, 15tr, 16tr, 17tr, 18tr, 19tr. **Royal Geographical Society**: 61c, 63c.

•

ELEMENTS OF PARKERS' ASTROLOGY PACK

INSTRUCTION BOOKLET: *Picture Credits*: **British Museum**: 1tl.

ASCENDANT CONCERTINA CHART: *Picture Credits*: **Bridgeman Art Library, London**: Victoria and Albert Museum, London tr; **Images Colour Library/Charles Walker Collection**: tl,bc.

MIDHEAVEN CONCERTINA CHART: *Picture Credits*: **Bridgeman Art Library, London**: Royal Geographic Society bc; **Images Colour Library/Charles Walker Collection**: tl, **Mary Evans Picture Library**: tr.

MOON CHARTS: *Picture Credits*: **Bridgeman Art Library, London**: Bibliothèque Nationale, Paris tl; British Library, London tr; **Sonia Halliday and Laura Lushington**: br; **Images Colour Library/Charles Walker Collection**: c, cr.

TRADITIONAL FACTORS: *Picture Credits*: **Bridgeman Art Library, London**: Victoria and Albert Museum, London tr; **Images Colour Library/Charles Walker Collection**: tl, bc; **Mary Evans Picture Library**: cl, cr.

PLANETARY TABLES: *Picture Credits*: **Bridgeman Art Library, London**: Bibliothèque Nationale, Paris 1bl; British Library, London 1br, 5c, 33cr; Museum of the History of Science, Oxford 2c; Victoria and Albert Museum, London 3c; **Sonia Halliday and Laura Lushington**: 1bc; **Images Colour Library/Charles Walker Collection**: 1tr, 42br, 45br; **Mary Evans Picture Library**: 11cr, 45br.

AIR WHEEL: *Picture Credits*: **Bruce Coleman**: Erich Crichton – Orchid; Kim Taylor – Swallow.

FIRE WHEEL: *Picture Credits*: **Planet Earth Pictures**: Nick Garbutt – Deer.

STICKER SHEETS: *Picture Credits*: **All Sport**: Athlete; **British Museum**: Chas Hawson, Money; **Coloursport**: Ice skater, Swimmer, Weightlifter; **Mary Evans Picture Library**: Boxer; **Food and Wine from France Ltd.**: Claret, Graves wine; **Robert Harding Picture Library**: Fencer; **Renault Communications**: Laguna; **Sopexa (UK) Ltd.**: Rose D'Anjou and Coupe. *Photography*: Peter Chadwick, Simon Clay, Andy Crawford, Liz McCauley, Philip Dowell, Geoff Dunn, Philip Gatward, Steve Gorton, Marc Henrie, Nicholas Hewetson, Dave King, John Lepine, David Murray, Stephen Oliver, Tim Ridley, Dave Rudkin, Guy Ryecart, Jules Selmes, Karl Shone, Clive Streeter, Harry Taylor, Kim Taylor, Matthew Ward, Barry Watts, Jerry Young. *Artwork*: Jane Thomson.

•

PLANETARY TABLES, MOON CHARTS, ASCENDANT *and* **MIDHEAVEN CHARTS**: *compiled by* John Filbey, D.F. Astrol. S.